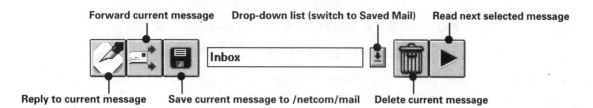

MAIL

Forward current message

Drop-down list (switch to Saved Mail)

Read next selected message

Inbox

Reply to current message

Save current message to /netcom/mail

Delete current message

NEWS

Reply with a message

Save current article to /netcom/news

Subscribe or unsubscribe to current newsgroup

Re-select the current article for re-reading

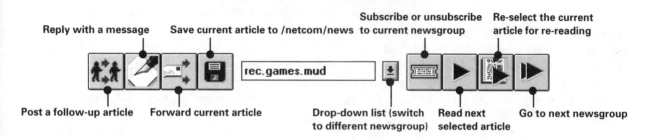

rec.games.mud

Post a follow-up article

Forward current article

Drop-down list (switch to different newsgroup)

Read next selected article

Go to next newsgroup

FTP

View a text or graphics file without downloading it

Upload a file

Current directory

Create a directory

/pub/sybex

a directory

Download a file

D1451067

GOPHER/WEB

Save the current document to disk

Find a word in the current document

Drop-down list of pages viewed this session (Web only)

Go to the previous document

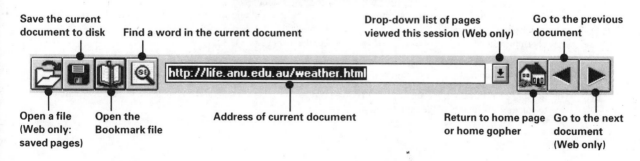

http://life.anu.edu.au/weather.html

Open a file (Web only: saved pages)

Open the Bookmark file

Address of current document

Return to home page or home gopher

Go to the next document (Web only)

For every kind of computer user, there is a SYBEX book.

All computer users learn in their own way. Some need straightforward and methodical explanations. Others are just too busy for this approach. But no matter what camp you fall into, SYBEX has a book that can help you get the most out of your computer and computer software while learning at your own pace.

Beginners generally want to start at the beginning. The **ABC's** series, with its step-by-step lessons in plain language, helps you build basic skills quickly. For a more personal approach, there's the **Murphy's Laws** and **Guided Tour** series. Or you might try our **Quick & Easy** series, the friendly, full-color guide, with **Quick & Easy References**, the companion pocket references to the **Quick & Easy** series. If you learn best by doing rather than reading, find out about the **Hands-On Live!** series, our new interactive multimedia training software. For hardware novices, there's the **Your First** series.

The **Mastering and Understanding** series will tell you everything you need to know about a subject. They're perfect for intermediate and advanced computer users, yet they don't make the mistake of leaving beginners behind. Add one of our **Instant References** and you'll have more than enough help when you have a question about your computer software. You may even want to check into our **Secrets & Solutions** series.

SYBEX even offers special titles on subjects that don't neatly fit a category—like our **Pushbutton Guides**, our books about the Internet, our books about the latest computer games, and a wide range of books for Macintosh computers and software.

SYBEX books are written by authors who are expert in their subjects. In fact, many make their living as professionals, consultants or teachers in the field of computer software. And their manuscripts are thoroughly reviewed by our technical and editorial staff for accuracy and ease-of-use.

So when you want answers about computers or any popular software package, just help yourself to SYBEX.

For a complete catalog of our publications, please write:

SYBEX Inc.
2021 Challenger Drive
Alameda, CA 94501
Tel: (510) 523-8233/(800) 227-2346 Telex: 336311
Fax: (510) 523-2373

SYBEX is committed to using natural resources wisely to preserve and improve our environment. As a leader in the computer book publishing industry, we are aware that over 40% of America's solid waste is paper. This is why we have been printing the text of books like this one on recycled paper since 1982.

This year our use of recycled paper will result in the saving of more than 15,300 trees. We will lower air pollution effluents by 54,000 pounds, save 6,300,000 gallons of water, and reduce landfill by 2,700 cubic yards.

In choosing a SYBEX book you are not only making a choice for the best in skills and information, you are also choosing to enhance the quality of life for all of us.

[1529] Access the Internet!

GET A FREE CATALOG JUST FOR EXPRESSING YOUR OPINION.

Help us improve our books and get a *FREE* full-color catalog in the bargain. Please complete this form, pull out this page and send it in today. The address is on the reverse side.

Name _____   **Company** _____

Address _____   **City** _____ **State** ____ **Zip** _____

Phone ( ) _____

1. How would you rate the overall quality of this book?
- ❑ Excellent
- ❑ Very Good
- ❑ Good
- ❑ Fair
- ❑ Below Average
- ❑ Poor

2. What were the things you liked most about the book? (Check all that apply)
- ❑ Pace
- ❑ Format
- ❑ Writing Style
- ❑ Examples
- ❑ Table of Contents
- ❑ Index
- ❑ Price
- ❑ Illustrations
- ❑ Type Style
- ❑ Cover
- ❑ Depth of Coverage
- ❑ Fast Track Notes

3. What were the things you liked *least* about the book? (Check all that apply)
- ❑ Pace
- ❑ Format
- ❑ Writing Style
- ❑ Examples
- ❑ Table of Contents
- ❑ Index
- ❑ Price
- ❑ Illustrations
- ❑ Type Style
- ❑ Cover
- ❑ Depth of Coverage
- ❑ Fast Track Notes

4. Where did you buy this book?
- ❑ Bookstore chain
- ❑ Small independent bookstore
- ❑ Computer store
- ❑ Wholesale club
- ❑ College bookstore
- ❑ Technical bookstore
- ❑ Other _____

5. How did you decide to buy this particular book?
- ❑ Recommended by friend
- ❑ Recommended by store personnel
- ❑ Author's reputation
- ❑ Sybex's reputation
- ❑ Read book review in _____
- ❑ Other _____

6. How did you pay for this book?
- ❑ Used own funds
- ❑ Reimbursed by company
- ❑ Received book as a gift

7. What is your level of experience with the subject covered in this book?
- ❑ Beginner
- ❑ Intermediate
- ❑ Advanced

8. How long have you been using a computer?
- years _____
- months _____

9. Where do you most often use your computer?
- ❑ Home
- ❑ Work

- ❑ Both
- ❑ Other _____

10. What kind of computer equipment do you have? (Check all that apply)
- ❑ PC Compatible Desktop Computer
- ❑ PC Compatible Laptop Computer
- ❑ Apple/Mac Computer
- ❑ Apple/Mac Laptop Computer
- ❑ CD ROM
- ❑ Fax Modem
- ❑ Data Modem
- ❑ Scanner
- ❑ Sound Card
- ❑ Other _____

11. What other kinds of software packages do you ordinarily use?
- ❑ Accounting
- ❑ Databases
- ❑ Networks
- ❑ Apple/Mac
- ❑ Desktop Publishing
- ❑ Spreadsheets
- ❑ CAD
- ❑ Games
- ❑ Word Processing
- ❑ Communications
- ❑ Money Management
- ❑ Other _____

12. What operating systems do you ordinarily use?
- ❑ DOS
- ❑ OS/2
- ❑ Windows
- ❑ Apple/Mac
- ❑ Windows NT
- ❑ Other _____

13. On what computer-related subject(s) would you like to see more books?

_____

_____

_____

_____

14. Do you have any other comments about this book? (Please feel free to use a separate piece of paper if you need more room)

_____

_____

_____

_____

PLEASE FOLD, SEAL, AND MAIL TO SYBEX

SYBEX INC.
Department M
2021 Challenger Drive
Alameda, CA
94501

Access the Internet!

David Peal

SYBEX®

San Francisco • Düsseldorf • Soest • Paris

Acquisitions Editor: Joanne Cuthbertson
Editors: David Krassner and Michelle Khazai
Technical Editor: Ingar Shu
Book Designer: Suzanne Albertson
Production Artist: Ingrid Owen
Screen Graphics: Ingrid Owen
Page Layout and Typesetting: Len Gilbert, Deborah Maizels, and Alissa Feinberg
Proofreader/Production Assistant: Emily Smith
Indexer: Ted Laux
Cover Designer: Ingalls + Associates
Cover Illustrator: Rebekah Lee

Library of Congress Card Number: 94-66406
ISBN: 0-7821-1529-2

Manufactured in the United States of America
10 9 8 7 6 5 4

For Carol, Gabriel, and Ella

Acknowledgments

A book on a huge topic cannot be created without a team. My debt to many is considerable. Where to start?

Bob Rieger, the owner and founder of Netcom and the visionary behind NetCruiser, generously supported this project from the beginning. John Whalen, the new president of Netcom, helped me manage the numerous operational and strategic details of a complex project. Rick Francis, the coordinator of the NetCruiser project, got me beta software to play with, personally answered countless questions, and helped review the manuscript. Peter Kaminski (known on the Internet for his list of Internet access providers, PDIAL), Roger Lian, and Jie Fu answered numerous questions as this project got started in earnest. Thanks to the whole Netcom development group for NetCruiser, a great product.

Erik Ingenito, Glee Harrah Cady, and Ken Brown came to my aid by drafting early sections of this book. Erik's inspired thoughts about Usenet give that chapter its energy and charm. Glee, author of NetCruiser's wonderful Help system, brings life to the uncharming world of anonymous FTP. Glee and Pete Kaminski read the entire book closely and offered many suggestions for improving it. Ken Brown, once a mentor and briefly a boss at Sybex, now a friend, did his best to make something out of the unforgiving substance of telnet.

Paul Hoffman, author of Sybex's peerless *Internet Instant Reference* (now you have to plug my book, Paul), was an integral player from the start, encouraging and admonishing me as he reviewed chapters. Thanks Paul. Bob Fasano, too, was a great support from the start.

Mail and Usenet News made it possible to get permissions for many of the illustrations in this book. For their generosity in granting permission I am grateful to the following people: Shari Steele, Director of Legal Services, Electronic Frontier Foundation; Ron Roeder, University of Texas; Stephen J. Smith; Frans van Hoesel; Steve Putz, Xerox PARC; Dr. Michael Greenhalgh, Australian National University, whose book on the Greek and Roman Cities of Western Turkey is about to become available (with 2,000 images) on the World Wide Web; Bill Britten, University of Tennessee (the lighthouse tour);Peter Plantec (Beverley Hills); Dr. David Green, Australian National University, for some great pages on the environment; Eric Johnson, University of Florida; Robert Guralnick, Museum of Paleontology, Berkeley; Win Treese, DEC's Cambridge Research Lab; Randee Exler and Scott W. Rogers, NASA's Goddard Space Flight Center; Amy Rebecca Ewing; Kevin Comerford, Dallas Museum of Art; Ron Hipschmann, Exploratorium; Stephen A. Spongberg, Arnold Aboretum, Harvard University; and Geoff Baehr. The image in Chapter 5 of the mosque in Peshawar is part of a collection of GIF images assembled by Asim Mughal and made available online as the Pakistan News Service Archives.

At Sybex, Rudolph Langer, Editor-in-Chief, encouraged me in the writing of this book, and Barbara Gordon, Managing Editor, offered quiet and considered support, with an eye on the schedule.

The people who actually did the work of making my ill-coded manuscript into an attractive book are David Krassner, my editor; Ingar Shu, technical editor; Len Gilbert, typesetter and fellow Internaut; Ingrid Owen, artist; Aldo Bermudez, screen graphics; and Emily Smith, proofreader and production assistant.

It was really my wonderful wife Carol Weiss who made this book possible. With much cool she did more than her share caring for Gabriel and Ella at the very time when she was making a major breakthrough in her research on HIV, thanks in part to new colleagues she communicates with daily over the Internet. As for Gabriel and Ella, this is their book, even though when they grow up they won't *need* computer books.

Contents at a Glance

Contents

CHAPTER 3

Usenet News: 6000 Points of Light

51

CHAPTER 4

Telnet: Long-Distance Computing

85

CHAPTER 5

FTP: Files to Go

109

CHAPTER 6

Dances with Gopher

139

CHAPTER 7

Web: The Best of the Net

171

Introduction

Nothing like the Internet has happened to desktop computing in years. It has opened up the world of the solitary individual pecking away at a word processor or database on a stand-alone machine, and made a reality of the old dream of a "world at your fingertips." But until now, the full Internet experience has been restricted to people with powerful computers and direct networked connections.

This book *gives* you the software that brings the experience of the Internet to you. NetCruiser, from Netcom Online Communications, provides on one disk everything you need to get started and go far. More important, it gives you everything you need to stay up to date on the Internet, where nothing stays put for long.

This Internet Book Is Different

This book is different from other Internet books because the NetCruiser software is different from the software you'll find in any other Internet book—or box. Only NetCruiser gives you all of the following:

- ◆ A direct connection to the Internet

- ◆ A Windows view of the online universe

- ◆ Software that upgrades itself online

- ◆ Access to the Internet via a national Internet access provider, Netcom

- ◆ All the tools you need to communicate with people, download files, use remote computers, browse the World Wide Web, and more

If you are not getting all these things, your access to the Internet is neither "full," nor "direct," nor very interesting to use or look at, nor likely to remain up to date for very long.

No piece of software is perfect. But because you can get new versions of NetCruiser free, online, the possibilities of incremental improvement are great. Who knows, maybe it will be perfect one day. That's what makes Netcom so important in the equation: Access to the Internet via Netcom gives you the means of continually updating the software. Appendix B tells you how the upgrade process works.

The book makes the software as easy to use as possible, by providing tips for using NetCruiser and for discovering the world of online resources.

Who This Book Is For

If you are new to the Internet, *Access the Internet!* makes using the Internet easier than using one of the commercial online services. Unlike other books, it provides you with everything you need. You don't have to shop for an access provider or hunt for additional applications.

If you have Internet experience on a PC, this software will probably mean a step up. If you have Internet experience on a powerful networked computer at work, this book and software will let you start having some fun at home as well.

If you are a current Netcom subscriber, you will want this book for the software and for the book's advice on using it effectively.

How This Book Is Organized

Books on the Internet are, roughly, divided into books about tools and books about resources. In addition, some books make access easier, although only this one has the software that provides every link of the chain from you to the Internet. *Access the Internet!* is a guide to using each of NetCruiser's six major tools to maximum advantage in finding and using Internet resources.

In this book, **resources** mean information available online—files, databases, people. A **tool** makes it possible to use specific resources.

The six tools you get with NetCruiser are

- ◆ mail
- ◆ Usenet News
- ◆ telnet
- ◆ FTP
- ◆ gopher
- ◆ World Wide Web

NetCruiser will be adding to this toolset as the months and years go by.

Chapter 1 tells you about the Internet and NetCruiser, and gives you a chance to try out your software. Each of Chapters 2–7 deals with one of the major tools. Each proceeds from a brief introduction to the tool and the way you use it in NetCruiser to an exploration of the resources the tool makes available to you. The choice of resources is pretty arbitrary, but each chapter gives you the means to locate resources of interest to you.

Chapter 2 (Mail) and Chapter 3 (Usenet News) introduce you to the Internet's most popular tools. Chapter 4 (Telnet) and Chapter 5 (FTP) are devoted to older tools that provide access to specific kinds of resources. Chapter 6 (Gopher) and Chapter 7 (World Wide Web) look at tools that provide easy-to-use interfaces and access to increasingly broad types of resources. These are the fun tools, and the growth areas of the Internet. Making them the last chapters of this book is a way of saving the best for last. You can read Chapters 2–7 in any order, but it's a good idea to start with Chapter 1.

Appendices A and B cover installing and updating your NetCruiser software.

Some Conventions

Where possible I have tried to make things easier by offering Tips, Warnings, and Notes based on my own experience with NetCruiser. Each has a special icon and is set off in special type.

A Tip gives you a shortcut or some advice.

 A Warning tells you what to avoid and, where possible, how to avoid it.

 A Note calls special attention to something that NetCruiser does, or provides a cross reference.

In step lists, when you are shown how to do something using a menu, you will see the following notation:

```
File ➤ Download new version
```

which means to go to the File menu and choose the *Download new version* option, using either the mouse or the keyboard.

 This book assumes you are comfortable using a mouse and Windows. Chapter 1 has some recommendations to make this easier.

Anything you see in **bold** is something you type. The individual keys you press to do something (such as q for quit) and the book's many computer addresses are set in regular type.

The asterisk (*) is a *wildcard,* which means it can stand for anything. In this book it is used whenever one part of an address or file name, for example, stays the same while another part (the wildcard) changes. For example, in Table 3.1 there is a description of a Usenet newsgroup called alt.current-events.*. This points you to a *family* of newsgroups all having to do with current events, such as alt.current-events.bosnia and alt.current-events.somalia.

Sometimes in Windows you must use more than one key to do something, such as make a menu selection. In this book two keys used together are joined by a plus sign (+). In Chapter 4, Ctrl+] means to hold down the Ctrl key and press the right bracket key. Common keystroke combinations are Ctrl+F4, to close a window (or a tool, such as mail or gopher), and Alt+F4, to end a NetCruiser session. F4 is *not* F+4, but a special key on your keyboard called a *function* key.

What Do You Think?

You can shape future editions of this book by sending me your comments, corrections, and suggestions. Send me e-mail, using NetCruiser, of course, at

`dpeal@ix.netcom.com`

Enjoy your travels, and stay in touch!

Up and Running in an Hour or So

Welcome! If you've never experienced the Internet, this book and the accompanying disk will get you started exploring the Internet's globe-spanning wealth of information—online books and magazines, electronic discussion groups, huge repositories of official records, software for Windows, DOS, and the Mac, you name it.

If you have some Internet experience using a PC, the software that comes with this book provides you with a direct, easy-to-use interface and powerful features that until recently have been available only to a few. The software is *NetCruiser*, a new Windows program created by Netcom, a national provider of Internet access, based in San Jose, California.

This chapter introduces the Internet and NetCruiser, then shows you how to use NetCruiser. Finally, you'll take NetCruiser for a test drive.

What Is the Internet, Anyway?

Before NetCruiser, you had to understand *how* the Internet worked to use it effectively. NetCruiser hides much of the complexity from you, so that, instead of learning about arcane things like TCP/IP and Unix, you can focus on what counts: finding information and exploring the immense resources available to you online. This book helps you both explore the Internet and manage its remaining complexity.

The Internet is two things: resources and tools for accessing them. The resources aren't just files, documents, and software, but *human* resources as well. You can find people who share your interests, who can answer your questions, who will play chess and backgammon with you (online of course), or who have just lived through an earthquake or revolution. Kids can find pen pals around the world, and lonely people can find solace (and perhaps a spouse, as happened to a friend of mine). The Internet currently reaches as many as 20 million people in more than 100 countries. The information available on the Internet is staggering in extent and scope. You'll learn about the *tools* a little later in this chapter in the section on NetCruiser. For now let's take a closer look at the Internet.

A Little Background

You'll get some insight into today's Internet if you realize that it was designed in the 1960s by the United States military to facilitate strategic communication—and to withstand nuclear attack. The Internet (then called the ARPANET, for the Department of Defense's Advanced Research Projects Agency) was designed to be highly decentralized. Even today, no central authority controls it, although organizations such as the Internet Society help devise standards to keep it running smoothly.

To accommodate the many different types of computers coming online, the Department of Defense wanted computers to be able to exchange information easily (that's why there's room on the Net for your PC). Networks had to be usable by computers with vastly different hardware configurations. The Internet today actually encompasses (without quite incorporating) many networks, such as NSFNET, BITNET, and Usenet, all of which you'll encounter later in this book. In addition, from the Internet you can easily communicate with people *outside* the Internet, on commercial networks such as CompuServe and America Online.

The early Internet was designed to divide information into data packets, then route the packets to their destination by the most efficient path, reassembling the information at the other end. Parts of the network that were not working could be easily avoided. Imagine driving on the interstate from New York to Boston. If your planned route through Hartford was blocked by an accident, you could take the highway through Providence instead. If both those routes were unavailable, you could take a third route, or a fourth.... That remains the principle for moving data on the Internet and a key to its ability to grow very fast.

Today you can almost always get where you're going on the Internet, but certain destinations are becoming so popular that the individual computers there cannot handle the demand (see Figure 1.1 for growth statistics).

The characteristics that made the ARPANET so valuable to the military also made the network that emerged in the 1970s and 1980s appealing to very different sorts of people: scientists, non-military researchers, teachers at every level, anarchists, hackers, and folks who flourish in an uncontrolled tumbleweed environment generally.

In the 1990s the big news is intense curiosity about the Internet on the part of business and the just-plain-curious. Despite the anti-corporate sentiments of the previous Net generation of the 1980s, more than half the new networks coming onto the Internet these days are businesses. The Internet promises new marketing and sales channels as well as improved lines of communication with consumers.

Things are changing fast: the Internet is increasingly teeming with entrepreneurs, its frontier culture is mingling with mainstream values, and government's guiding role is yielding to corporate influence. For technical reasons, the Internet is big enough for everybody—government bureaucrats, countercultural groups of every sort, entrepreneurs, researchers, even normal people.

What Is NetCruiser?

NetCruiser is software that connects you to the new frontier that is the Internet. It provides you with

- ◆ A direct connection that actually makes your computer part of the Internet
- ◆ A friendly Windows interface

Annual rate of growth for Gopher traffic: 997%
◆
Annual rate of growth for World-Wide Web traffic: 341,634% (1st year)
◆
Number of countries reachable by electronic mail: 137 (approx.)
◆
Number of countries not reachable by electronic mail: 99 (approx.)
◆
Number of countries on the Internet: 60
◆
Average time between new networks connecting to the Internet: 10 minutes
◆
Number of newspaper and magazine articles about the Internet during the first nine months of 1993: over 2300
◆
Number of mail messages carried by IBM's Internet gateways in January, 1993: about 340,000
◆
Number of mail messages carried by Digital's Internet gateways in June, 1993: over 700,000
◆
Advertised network numbers in October, 1993: 16,533
◆
Advertised network numbers in October, 1992: 7,505
◆
Date after which more than half the registered networks were commercial: August, 1991
◆
Number of USENET articles posted in two weeks in December, 1993: 605,000
◆
Number of megabytes of USENET articles posted: 1450
◆
Number of users posting USENET articles: 130,000
◆
Number of USENET sites represented: 42,000
◆
Number of on-line coffeehouses in San Francisco: 18
◆
Cost for four minutes of Internet time at those coffeehouses: $0.25
◆
Date on which first Stephen King short story published via the Internet before print publication: 19 September 1993
◆
Round-trip time from Digital CRL to mcmvax.mcmurdo.gov in McMurdo, Antarctica: 640 milliseconds
◆
Amount of time it takes for Supreme Court decisions to become available on the Internet: less than one day.
◆
Date of first National Public Radio program broadcast simultaneously on the Internet: 21 May 1993

FIGURE 1.1: Amazing facts about the Net, courtesy of Win Treese

◆ Physical access to the Internet via Netcom, a national Internet provider

◆ A full set of tools for exploring the Internet's resources

NetCruiser Gives You...A Direct Internet Connection

NetCruiser gives you a *direct* connection to the Internet. Even though you get onto the Internet using a modem, with a direct connection you have your own address on the Internet, and files you download are sent directly to your machine.

 The technical term for this direct connection is **SLIP**, short for Serial-Line Internet Protocol. Until recently, SLIP has not been widely used because of the price of the service and the difficulty of configuring it. NetCruiser is the first product to make SLIP accessible and easy to use, and Netcom is one of a handful of access providers to make a direct connection affordable.

A direct connection isn't much use in itself. What's important is that a direct connection makes it possible to communicate as a peer with all the other computers on the Net. The direct connection also makes it possible to use several Internet tools at once, something you'll come to appreciate.

...A Graphical Interface (It's Easy to Use)

NetCruiser puts a friendly Windows interface on the sometimes hostile Internet—see Figure 1.2.

With its point-and-click simplicity, Windows helps you cut through the complexity of the Internet—see Figure 1.3.

Character-Based vs. Graphical Interfaces

The vast majority of Internet users still use programs with *character-based* interfaces, which means that you see only characters on your screen (no

```
                                    Weather & global monitoring (p1 of 3)

                    [IMAGE] WEATHER & GLOBAL MONITORING

    The following information is available via ANU Bioinformatics
    Hypermedia Service
    _____

      * Current weather satellite images, including
            + Australia (most recent)
            + Pacific hemisphere (most recent)
            + USA (infrared)
            + Atlantic hemisphere
            + Japan, China & Korea
            + Current US weather maps & movies: via MSU, and via NIH
            + Current European weather images (via UK)
            + GMS weather satellite images (FTP to Archie)
      * Weather reports and forecasts
            + Australia (telnet to Bureau of Meteorology)
            + Australia (gopher to Bureau of Meteorology)
            + Canada
    -- press space for next page --
     Arrow keys: Up and Down to move. Right to follow a link; Left to go back.
    H)elp O)ptions P)rint G)o M)ain screen Q)uit /=search [delete]=history list
```

FIGURE 1.2: Then...The World Wide Web's character-based interface

graphics, buttons, scroll bars, and so on). These programs work with any connection to the Internet, and are therefore the most widely used. A few of the popular programs, such as the Unix mail program and the file-transfer protocol, FTP, are *line-oriented* programs, meaning the commands and the results of the commands scroll up your screen a line at a time. More modern programs, such as gopher, are *screen-oriented*, meaning they assume that you have an 80-by-24 character screen, and commands and results appear in different parts of the screen. Most people find screen-oriented programs easier to use than line-oriented programs.

NetCruiser brings that full-screen orientation to your PC, and is graphical as well, meaning you can use your mouse and familiar Windows actions instead of relying on your keyboard.

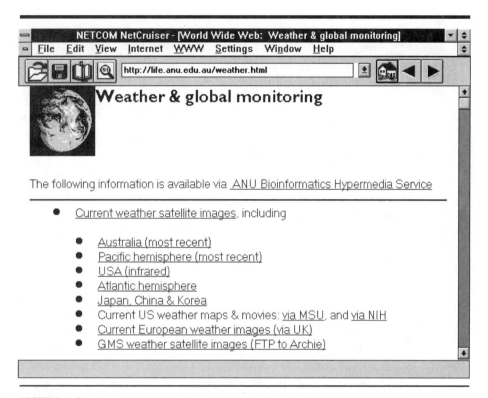

The following information is available via ANU Bioinformatics Hypermedia Service

- Current weather satellite images, including
    - Australia (most recent)
    - Pacific hemisphere (most recent)
    - USA (infrared)
    - Atlantic hemisphere
    - Japan, China & Korea
    - Current US weather maps & movies: via MSU, and via NIH
    - Current European weather images (via UK)
    - GMS weather satellite images (FTP to Archie)

FIGURE 1.3: Now…NetCruiser's graphical interface to the World Wide Web

…The Convenience and Value of Netcom

Even though NetCruiser makes your Internet connection direct, you still need an Internet access provider to get onto the Internet. Netcom, the creator of NetCruiser, makes this service available at a competitive monthly fee. Netcom has *points of presence* across the country. From most metropolitan areas, Internet access is a local call away. A city's point of presence is a computer attached to a bank of modems and connected to the site of the host computer, which in turn is connected to the Internet. Access across the country sets Netcom apart from the many service providers who are available in only one area code (617 or 206, say).

Because of today's high-speed digital networks, it's more important to have a reliable and low-cost access provider than one that is located across the street. With Netcom you get reliable and low-cost service as well as many points of presence. Netcom is constantly adding new points of presence (see Appendix B for a way to find out about them), and is currently expanding into small cities as well as Canada.

Another important feature of the NetCruiser service is that it allows you to use fast modems (currently, up to 38.4kb per second). With data compression, you can actually transfer certain kinds of data at a multiple of this speed.

 With a direct connection to the Internet, the faster the modem, the better the performance: Your commands are carried out faster and results come to your computer faster. Make sure, too, that your modem supports both error correction (v.42) and data compression (v.42bis). Speed and compression improve data **throughput**—the amount of data transported to and from your computer per second.

NetCruiser Updates Itself Automatically

One of the most exciting features of NetCruiser is that future versions of the software, bringing you new features or improvements of existing features, are available to you by a simple point and click. To take advantage of this feature, choose Download New Version from the File menu after you log on to NetCruiser. See Appendix B for procedures on keeping NetCruiser software up to date.

...Tools for Finding a Needle in the Internet

The millions of files, thousands of online conferences, and terabytes of data (that's a thousand gigabytes, each of which is a thousand megabytes!) that have been deposited on the Internet over the last two decades, and that continue to accumulate as you are reading this paragraph, aren't much good without tools for locating exactly what you're looking for. Even if you're interested in browsing (as most people are), tools can make it easier to explore the library of Internet resources, then linger when you've found something of interest, such as discussion groups about gamelan music, child care, computer programming, taxes, or hang-gliding. The NetCruiser software you get with this book gives you Windows versions of the most important *tools* on the Internet:

- ◆ Mail
- ◆ Usenet news
- ◆ Telnet
- ◆ FTP
- ◆ Gopher
- ◆ A World Wide Web graphical browser

Electronic Mail: I and Thou (and the Rest of Us)

The fastest growing category of PC software today is *electronic mail* (e-mail). While the first generation of PC software emphasized productivity tools that made individuals work more efficiently by themselves, e-mail software for networks is now helping people work more efficiently with other people. Electronic mail is good for more than human communication; in later chapters you'll learn how to use mail to query databases and download files.

On the Internet the Unix mail program has long been the most common and widely used e-mail tool. With NetCruiser's easy-to-use mailer, you'll be able to communicate with just about anyone, just about anywhere (although like most people, you'll probably be sending messages to a handful of friends, co-workers, and bosses). You'll also be able to join organized mailing lists, and take part in online discussions with groups of people with shared interests. You'll learn more about mail and mailing lists in Chapter 2.

Usenet News: The World's Town Square

After mail, the most popular tool on the Internet is Usenet news. Currently, there are more than 6,000 online discussion groups on every subject from Barney to robotics—actually, including very small and regional newsgroups there are more than 8,000 newsgroups! Usenet news lets you read and post *articles* about any subject, and other people anywhere on the Internet can read and reply to them. You can find discussions about politics, computer systems, religion, almost every profession, how-to's for almost anything, music, recreation, science, and so on. You'll learn more about Usenet news in Chapter 3.

Telnet: Tapping Resources on Remote Computers

Telnet is a tool that lets you log on to and use remote computers (*remote* is computer jargon for *somebody else's*). What sort of resources? Libraries, for one thing—hundreds of them. The Library of Congress Information System (LOCIS), for instance, is available via telnet, as are local libraries with harder-to-find titles in their collections. You can also use telnet to play interactive games like Go and Scrabble, as you'll see in Chapter 4.

FTP: Helping Yourself to Files

FTP, the *file transfer protocol*, is a standard that defines how computers connect and transfer files; the Internet's File Transfer Program does the work of transferring files. NetCruiser's FTP tool helps you communicate with computers (not people), and most of the conversation is one-way; it's more common to *download* files from another computer than to *upload* them to it. Millions of files are available on the Internet through FTP, and some of them you will want to have for your own use. Using FTP you can get plain text files (which *you* read) as well as binary files (e.g., programs for *your computer* to run). You can read about FTP in Chapter 5.

Gopher: Burrowing for Gold

Since 1991, a new tool called *gopher* has made it much easier to use resources of all sorts on different computers. Instead of typing in commands to open "sessions" with a remote computer, with gopher you deal with a hierarchical menu of numbered resources. Using NetCruiser all you have to do is click the resource you want. To learn all about gopher (and to find out where the word comes from), read Chapter 6. You'll also get a taste of gopher later in this chapter.

World Wide Web: The Internet Just Got Easier

Internet tools are getting easier to use all the time; the Web presents the best Internet resources in a *hypertext* format: you click highlighted words and images in Web *pages* and go directly to related information throughout the world. The Web is not only a repository of data on which users have imposed some order; it also gives you alternative access to other tools, such as FTP and gopher. In the future you can expect to see the Web encompassing more tools and making more resources available on the Net. This whole topic is saved for the last chapter of this book.

What's in the Toolbox?

Netcom has brought these tools together in a way that simplifies access to them all, makes them easy to use, and allows them to be used together—even at the same time.

Some of the tools you get with NetCruiser make it possible for you to communicate with people (mail and Usenet news). Others facilitate communication with computers, so that you can download files or use remote resources (FTP and telnet).

What's special about gopher and Web is that they take your perspective, not the network's, and make it easier to specify *what* you are looking for. These newer tools can also be customized. Once you've found interesting resources with gopher and the Web (as well as with Usenet), it's easy to mark them and go directly to them in the future. NetCruiser makes even the older tools easier to use by helping you keep track of FTP and telnet addresses, then select them up from easy-to-use lists, rather than from memory. You'll also discover that gopher and Web are not only easy to use, but make it easier to use older Internet tools like FTP.

Using NetCruiser

You install NetCruiser as you would any Windows program: put the disk in your drive, select File ➤ Run, and run NetCruiser's Setup program, answering questions as you are prompted to do so. If you need help, Appendix A guides you through the installation process. NetCruiser technical support is available from Netcom at 1-408-983-1510.

Using a Couple of Programs at Once under Windows

With Windows, you can use more than one program at the same time. In NetCruiser, this means that if someone recommends a gopher site in a mail message, you can click on the gopher button to visit the gopher site, then send mail to the person who recommended the site. All three tools—Read Mail, Send Mail, and Gopher—can be running at the same time, and you can switch between them by clicking on the Window menu and selecting from the bottom of the menu. (They are numbered, so all you have to do is press the number of the tool to use it.) Also, you can cycle between NetCruiser and *other* open Windows programs by pressing Alt+Tab. To open another application, you press Alt+Tab until you come to the Program Manager, find the icon for the application you want to use, and double-click. You could use this feature to explore with gopher, then write up your results in your favorite word processor (as I am doing now).

Logging On

You run NetCruiser by double-clicking on its icon in the NETCOM Program Group.

NetCruiser

A dialog box displays the Username you chose when you registered the program (see Figure 1.4).

There is also a line for you to enter your password. Type your password and press Enter or click Start Login to connect to Netcom's computer.

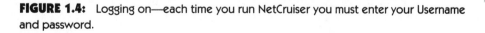

FIGURE 1.4: Logging on—each time you run NetCruiser you must enter your Username and password.

Both your Username and password are case-sensitive. If you capitalize a letter that should be small, you'll be unable to log on. If you get an error message indicating you typed the wrong password, double-check your Username too: errors in either the Username or the password trigger the incorrect password error message.

NetCruiser now starts the process of logging on. Logging on is not instantaneous: NetCruiser must first "find" your modem, dial into Netcom, log on to Netcom, get you an IP address (more about IP addresses in Chapter 2), and start your *session*. These steps are monitored in the title bar (the top) of your NetCruiser log-on window. Press Stop Login if you get a busy signal and want to try another phone number, or if any step of the login process takes too long. Press Start Login to try again. If you are unable to log in at all, exit NetCruiser (double-click the Control box or press Alt+F4) and try again later.

⬤ Getting Your Bearings

When you log on successfully, the dialog box goes away, and you see Net-Cruiser's main window (or application window, as it's called in Windows terminology), a globe and the Netcom banner (Figure 1.5).

This books assumes you are comfortable using a mouse and Windows. If you're not, take some time to learn how your mouse works, select from menus, change the size of windows, minimize and maximize windows, and switch between programs. You might want to read a good book about Windows, such as **Murphy's Laws of Windows**, also from SYBEX.

Figure 1.5 shows you the nerve center from which you use tools and explore resources. Whenever you use one of NetCruiser's tools, you are using a *document window* within the main window. Note that a document window is always contained in an application window.

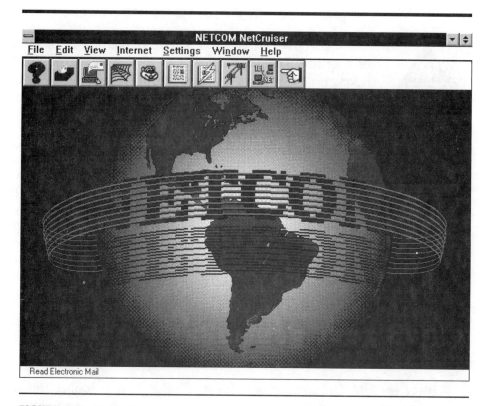

FIGURE 1.5: NetCruiser's main window—you can select a tool by clicking on a toolbar icon or selecting from the Internet menu.

Here are the most important elements of your NetCruiser display.

Menus The menus (along the top of the screen) let you use your mouse or keyboard to select commands—such as the command to download a document or to change the font you're using in World Wide Web. You'll learn about specific menu commands as they come up in the book. Whenever a menu name is underlined on your screen, you can open the menu by pressing the Alt key together with the underlined letter. On an open menu, you can launch a command by simply pressing the underlined key. Using the mouse, you click on the menu name, then click and release on the command name.

Most tools have one or two menus that are unique to them. The tool-specific menus provide an alternative method to clicking on the **toolbar buttons** that you'll see when you use that tool. For example, when you use World Wide Web, you'll see the WWW menu, which gives you the same capabilities as the WWW toolbar.

Toolbar The toolbar just below the menus on the main window shows you a series of box-shaped icons (little pictures), each representing an Internet tool. To use the tool, just click the box. (You'll learn later, however, that there can be several paths to the same tool on the Internet itself; you can, for instance, get to gopher from within World Wide Web.) The Internet menu provides the same functions as the toolbar, if you prefer to use a menu. Most tools have their own toolbars, allowing you to do such things as move around and save a document.

Internet Site Chooser When you start telnet, FTP, or gopher, the first thing you see is a map of the United States. As you move your mouse around the map without clicking, you'll notice that states' names appear in a box in the lower right. Clicking within a state displays a *drop-down list* of addresses for that state. (You'll learn about addresses in Chapter 2.) To see the whole list, click on the downward-pointing arrow and use your mouse or arrow keys to scroll down the list. You can either select a site from the list or type an address directly into the Site box on the toolbar. Click on Canada to select a site *anywhere* outside the U.S.

Status Bar When you're actually using a tool, a context-sensitive *status bar* appears at the bottom of the window. The left side of the status line shows you the name of whatever screen element or document your mouse is traversing (and the names zip by quickly). When you are moving from site to site or transferring files from computer to computer, the right side of the status bar keeps track of the amount of data being transferred (in bytes). The appearance of and the information in the status line differ from tool to tool, but this is the place to look when you want to see what's going on at any moment. It's especially useful to monitor data transfers—data being downloaded from the Internet to your computer. Here's a message you might see while using the Usenet newsgroup reader:

(getting headers 3068-3168...)		3072

Removing the toolbar or status bar from view (View ➤ Toolbar or View ➤ Status Bar) gives you more room, which can be handy if you are using a tool such as Web that displays a great deal of information. (The ➤ symbol indicates a menu choice.) You can use the Internet menu instead of the toolbar if the toolbar isn't displayed.

Help Whenever you have a question about what something does while you are working, you can use NetCruiser's built-in Help system. You use the Help system by selecting Help from the menu bar or by clicking the Help icon (the question mark) on the toolbar. The following Help menu items are expecially useful:

Menu	What It Has
Contents	A description of the major features of the program, with useful background information about mail and the other tools.
Search	To search for specific topics, such as IP addresses. The information is the same as you'll find under Contents, but it is organized at a "lower level," so you can zero in on topics of interest to you.

Wherever you are in Help, clicking on a word that's underlined and in a different color brings up a definition of the word or a fuller explanation.

This way of linking information is called *hypertext*, and is a simpler version of what you'll find on a global scale in World Wide Web—a method of linking information to related information.

One of the best features of Netcom's Help system is the listings of interesting places to visit on the Internet. The listings are a good place to start if you want to explore.

Taking a Test Cruise

Let's take NetCruiser for a trial cruise. This little exercise has an ulterior motive: it shows that the Internet itself is often the best source of information about the Internet—it's one big help system. You'll also learn a little about gopher, a simple menu-driven Internet tool that you'll learn much more about in Chapter 6.

A Caveat and a Commitment Everything in the Internet is subject to change. Resources move, maintainers of resources get new jobs, tools are refined, new tools are invented, computer addresses change; only the Internet remains, but flexibility, rapid growth, and volatility are its defining characteristics. Remember this truism as you read about specific resources in this book. Most chapters give you advice for using the Internet itself to keep up to date with the Internet. For example, to keep up with FTP resources, there's a utility called archie (Chapter 5). For gopher resources, there's—you guessed it, veronica (Chapter 6). NetCruiser software will help you keep up with changes in the Internet through periodic software upgrades—whenever they are required. You can find instructions for upgrading your copy of NetCruiser in Appendix B.

Follow these steps to get access to a very useful online book about the Internet:

1. From Windows' Program Manager, double-click on the NetCruiser icon. Log on to NetCruiser by entering your password and pressing ↵. After you log on successfully, you'll see the main window (*application window*) of the NetCruiser program (Figure 1.5).

2. On the button bar, click on the gopher button

   The Site Browser (a map of the United States) comes up.

3. In the Site box at the top of the map, type in **gopher.eff.org.** You'll learn about addresses in Chapter 2. For now note that *eff* is the acronym for the Electronic Frontier Foundation, which is an organization (hence .org). You'll see the menu shown in Figure 1.6.

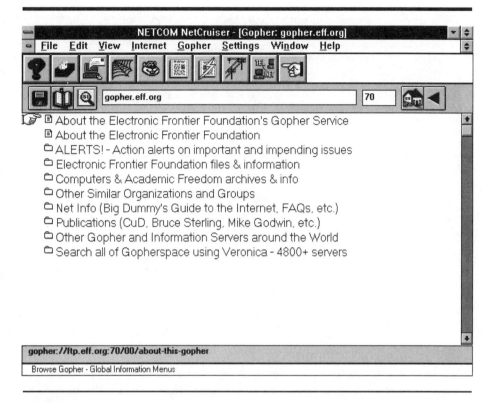

FIGURE 1.6:   The top level gopher menu at gopher.eff.org—double-clicking on any of the folders takes you a level lower. This menu is subject to change.

4. First, choose *Net Info* by double-clicking. A new menu comes up (Figure 1.7). Notice that each of the menu entries is preceded by a little picture (*icon*). A folder *contains* things: either documents you can read, or more folders. When you see a document icon instead of a folder, you are at the bottom of the hierarchy. Now choose EFF's Guide to the Internet.

5. From the new menu, double-click FAQ (Frequently Asked Questions). A FAQ is a good place to start whenever you are exploring a new subject or resource on the Internet.

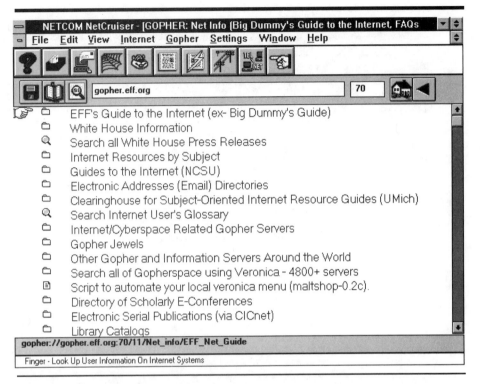

FIGURE 1.7: A gopher menu can display folders (menus), readable text documents, downloadable graphics files, and more. Each kind of item has its own icon. You'll learn all about the things you can find in a gopher den in Chapter 6.

6. Get an overview of the contents of *EFF's Guide to the Internet* (formerly the *Big Dummy's Guide*). You can get around the document using the scroll bar and mouse, the PageUp and PageDown keys, and the arrow keys. When you're done, click the left-pointing button on the toolbar to return to the menu. If you are curious about a particular Internet subject, then read the ASCII version of the *Guide* itself (Figure 1.8). Otherwise, you can return to the EFF main menu by clicking on the Home button on gopher's toolbar, use another tool (such as mail), or leave gopher either by pressing Ctrl+F4 or double-clicking on the Control menu in the upper-left corner of the gopher window.

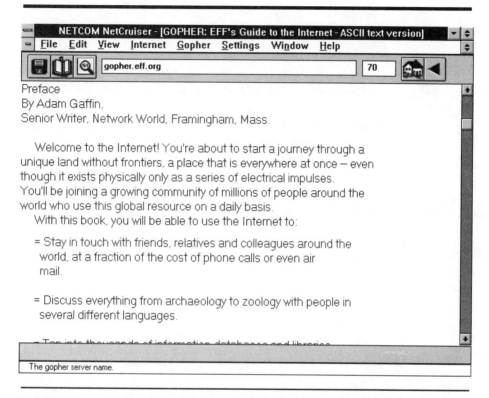

NETCOM NetCruiser - [GOPHER: EFF's Guide to the Internet - ASCII text version]

File   Edit   View   Internet   Gopher   Settings   Window   Help

gopher.eff.org   70

Preface
By Adam Gaffin,
Senior Writer, Network World, Framingham, Mass.

Welcome to the Internet! You're about to start a journey through a unique land without frontiers, a place that is everywhere at once — even though it exists physically only as a series of electrical impulses. You'll be joining a growing community of millions of people around the world who use this global resource on a daily basis.
With this book, you will be able to use the Internet to:

= Stay in touch with friends, relatives and colleagues around the world, at a fraction of the cost of phone calls or even air mail.

= Discuss everything from archaeology to zoology with people in several different languages.

The gopher server name.

FIGURE 1.8:   Here's a sample page from **EFF's Guide to the Internet**. In later chapters you'll learn how to search documents online and to download documents to your computer.

EFF's Guide to the Internet is an online book about the Internet that was written by Adam Gaffin and published by the Electronic Frontier Foundation, a group that works to protect civil rights on the Internet and throughout the "virtual" world.

Just because something's available online doesn't mean that it is not copyrighted or that you can freely use and adapt it as you wish. A document must be explicitly placed in the public domain for you to redistribute it freely. Otherwise, it's best to assume that it's copyrighted. It's a good idea to clear the status of a document before using it, especially for commercial purposes.

This long, informative, online book is presented as a series of sections devoted to special Internet topics—such as Gopher and Mail.

One of the beauties of "publishing" documents such as the **EFF's Guide to the Internet** online is that they can be updated more easily and often than is in the case with print media. A March 1994 revision of this guide is available at gopher.eff.org. Burrow and you'll find this document, and more.

Exiting NetCruiser

When you are finished with NetCruiser for the day (you may soon find yourself staying up late playing with the product), exit using one of the following standard Windows techniques:

◆ Press Alt+F4

◆ Select File ➤ Exit

◆ Double-click on the Control menu icon (the little box with a big dash through it), in the upper-left corner of the main window

Your modem switches off automatically if it is internal. Otherwise, turn it off by hand.

You've Just Begun

You've now read about the Internet, heard some praise for NetCruiser, and maybe poked around a gopher den. The best way to really get to know the Internet is to explore it on your own, in all its breadth and depth. The following chapters give you pointers for finding what you are looking for on the Internet. You can read them in order, or just read the ones you need.

The focus of this book is on the tools NetCruiser gives you. Finding information or meeting people may be what drew you to the Internet, but good exploring requires sharp tools, expertly used. Happy hunting!

It's in the Mail

E-mail has been an integral part of the Internet from the beginning, enabling friends, generals, colleagues, bosses, hobbyists, and others to communicate with each other from a distance. The Unix mail program was for years the most common way of exchanging e-mail, but it had an interface so user-unfriendly that you couldn't edit a line once you'd finished it. Two common Unix mail programs, elm and Pine, offer easier interfaces and more features than mail, but also suffer the lingering restrictions of a character-based interface.

The NetCruiser mailer gives you a simple graphical editor for composing and reading messages to send to other people. As in any Windows program, you can cut and paste within and between documents to make it easier to edit your message. Mail is perhaps the most useful tool on the Internet; for millions it has become an essential part of daily life. This chapter

♦ Introduces e-mail addresses.

♦ Shows you how to use the NetCruiser mailer to send, receive, and manage your messages.

♦ Gives you some tips for finding addresses.

♦ Shows you how to exchange mail with people on networks other than the Internet.

◆ Introduces mailing lists, so you can keep in touch with colleagues and experts in your field and with people around the world who share your interests.

Anatomy of an Address

To receive mail, other people must have your address; to send mail, you need theirs. Your Internet mailing address contains your user name, an @ symbol, and the name of the computer (sometimes called the *domain name*) on which your account resides (netcom.com, say).

User Name The first part of your address is easy: it's the name you chose when you registered NetCruiser (see Appendix A). Most names are short, eight characters or fewer. Internet names never have spaces in them and are, by Unix convention, all lowercase letters. No two accounts on a computer have the same name.

Computer Name The computer-name part of an address is a bit more complex. Every computer name on the Internet has at least one period in it, and many have two or three. The period, commonly pronounced *dot* when the name is spoken, separates the parts of the computer address. The left-most part of the computer address is the name of the computer; the right-most part of the address is called the top-level domain; it defines the computer's location or the type of organization it belongs to. From left to right your computer is included in ever-wider categories.

This whole system is called the Domain Name System. From time to time you'll encounter a numeric address, such as 128.218.1.14 (a computer in the University of California at San Francisco domain). This is the Internet Protocol (IP) address, which defines a computer's physical location on the Internet, and is used in routing data. The IP address is also organized in hierarchical fashion, except in reverse order. The IP address always appears as four numbers separated by periods. Starting on the left, the numbers represent the network you're part of, the subnetwork, and the specific computer.

On the Internet, the top-level domain names are standardized so that mail can be routed easily. There are two types of domain names: *descriptive* and *geographical*. Descriptive names tell the type of organization the computer belongs to (such as *gov* for government); the geographical names tell the location of the computer (such as *de* for Deutschland). A computer address usually has one type of domain name.

Here are the most common descriptive domain names:

Name	Description	Example
com	Commercial businesses	netcom.com
edu	Educational institutions	itsa.ucsf.edu
gov	Federal government	whitehouse.gov
mil	U.S. military	nctamslant.navy.mil
org	Miscellaneous organizations	yukon.cren.org
net	Organizations administering a network	ds.internic.net

The geographical names are always two-letter country abbreviations, such as *ca* for Canada (not California!) and *jp* for Japan.

Top-level "descriptive" domain names aren't reliably descriptive. Many network access providers (such as Netcom) do not have "net" as their top-level domain name, and a computer with a top-level domain name of "edu" may be used for commercial or military purposes. To further complicate things, there is no standard way of deciding whether the top level should be descriptive or geographical.

Using NetCruiser Mail

NetCruiser's mail program is the heart of much of what you will do on the Internet. You can use it to communicate with individuals around the world. You can also use it to stay up to date on any of thousands of subjects and to meet experts and enthusiasts in just about any field that interests you. The raw material of e-mail is the message. Each mail message consists of two parts: the header and the content, and the NetCruiser Read Mail window is arranged accordingly.

Anatomy of a Message

The *header* is all the information a normal person needs, in most cases. Here's the information you get in the header of every message you receive using NetCruiser:

Message: message number, sequentially from 1, beginning with the oldest message

To: your e-mail address (*login@computer.address*)

From: who sent the message (e-mail address plus real name in parentheses)

Subject: what the message is about, as characterized by the sender

Date: when it was sent; automatically determined

Much of the apparent garbage in the headers of old-style Unix mail messages (such as the path the message took, the message number, and the programs used in delivering it) in fact provided diagnostic information that network experts could evaluate if something went wrong. That information is still there, but NetCruiser shields you from it. When you reply to or forward a message (more about that later), you can see a Unix message header in all its glory.

The message itself is referred to as the *body*.

Reading Your Mail

Reading mail is not just a matter of reading your *new* mail, it also involves reviewing your old mail, replying to and forwarding mail, and managing your mail—deleting and storing messages. Start by selecting Internet ➤ Read Mail-In or click on the Read Mail icon in the toolbar:

The Select a Folder window opens. Select the *type* of message to read, In-box or Saved Mail.

Inbox	New messages as well as old messages you have not saved
Saved Mail	Messages you have already read, and have saved by pressing the Save button

The Read Mail window comes up right away (see Figure 2.1). Your system now connects to the Netcom mail server (sort of like a Post Office), then downloads and displays all the message *headers* of the messages in the category you chose (Inbox or Saved Mail). At any time while using Inbox or Saved Mail, you can switch to the other category using the drop-down box.

Using the Read Mail Window

The Read Mail window has two *panes* (yes, the parts of a window are its panes). The upper pane displays headers from all your messages (see Figure 2.2).

The header shows a number for each message, with the oldest message having the lowest number (*1*). For each message, you can see the sender's address, name (in parentheses), and subject (from the message's Subject line, abridged to fit on one line). You open a message (read it in the pane below) by double-clicking a header.

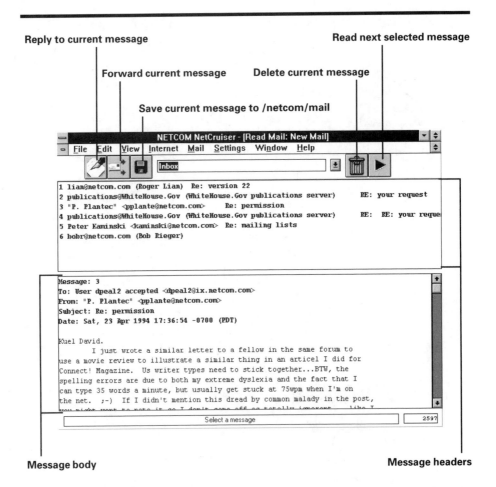

Reply to current message

Forward current message

Delete current message

Read next selected message

Save current message to /netcom/mail

Message body

Message headers

FIGURE 2.1: The Read Mail: New Mail window

```
18 publications@WhiteHouse.Gov (WhiteHouse.Gov publications server)
19 Glee Harrah Cady <glee@netcom.com>   correction to last email
20 Glee Harrah Cady <glee@netcom.com>   Internaut V1 N1 now available
21 rickf@netcom.com (Rick Francis)      Re: web
```

FIGURE 2.2: The headers displayed in the Read Mail window, showing sequence, sender, and subject

The lower pane is where you'll see the body of the message you've selected in the upper pane; it is blank until you have opened a message to read. A scroll bar appears for either pane if the list of messages or the message itself is too long to appear in the pane.

A double line separates the two panes. To resize either pane, move your mouse over the double line until it turns into a double arrow (pointing up and down) and simply drag (click and hold down) the border between the panes until the relative size of the panes is just right for you. Similarly you can resize the window as a whole by dragging a side or a corner of the window.

It's a good idea to maximize your mailer (click on the upward-pointing triangle in the upper-right of the window) so you can see both panes at the same time. Resize the panes to exclude the pane you're not using or to show just the part of it you need.

Managing Your Mail

If you subscribe to mailing lists (more about them later in this chapter), you'll appreciate NetCruiser Mail's built-in utilities for helping you manage your messages:

◆ Disposing of unwanted mail (alas not automatically, yet)

◆ Replying to the person who sent you the message

◆ Forwarding the message to someone else

The buttons at the top of the Read Mail window make message-management easier than it was using the old Unix mail program.

Reply Lets you send a message to someone who has sent a message to you. When you choose Reply, you get a choice of whether to include the original message. If you do, the text is "quoted"—each line is set off by a greater than sign (>). Replies are automatically addressed to the original sender, and the subject is the same as in the original message. You can change the subject by editing it, and add addresses by pressing the To... button. Click Send when your reply is complete.

Forward If you think others should see a message, *forward* it. Selecting Forward brings up NetCruiser's Address Mail To... window, which you can read more about in the "Sending Messages" section. When you forward, you can include people to cc or Bcc. After you select an address or addresses and click OK, the Send Mail window comes up with the forwarding address(es) you selected. You can edit the addresses by clicking on the To... button. You can also summarize the "quoted" message you are forwarding and add your own comments where appropriate. When done, click Send.

Save A message on your hard disk to keep a record of it. When you save a message, it is automatically stored in the \netcom\mail directory created by NetCruiser during installation. The message becomes a file with an eight-digit file name and extension of .msg (starting at 00000001.msg). You can read old messages using File ➤ View Text File.... With a word processor you can open messages and save them with meaningful names.

Delete One or more selected messages. Choose Mail ➤ Undelete to restore deleted messages.

Display The next selected message.

Printing a Message To print a message that is displayed, just select File ➤ Print Message.

Sending Messages

Sending messages is simpler than receiving them, especially since much of the message-sending you will do is automatically handled by the Reply and Forward capabilities of the Read Mail window; replying to a message, or forwarding it, automatically sends it on its way.

To send a message, select Internet ➤ Send Mail-Out or click on the Send Mail icon:

The Address Mail To... window now comes up (Figure 2.3). (You'll also see this window when you forward a mail message or Usenet article.) Enter the address of the recipient by typing it directly into the field in the top left of the window (Enter Email Address Here...). Or, if the address is in your Address Book, select an address from the Choose Address From Address Book box in the lower left. (See "Keeping an Address Book.")

It's in the Mail

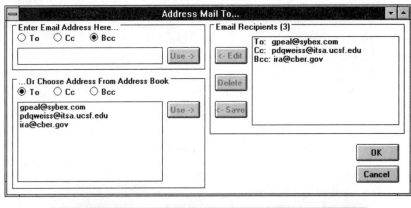

FIGURE 2.3: Use the Address Mail To… window (top) to specify one or more recipients of your message (To), as well as other people you want to receive the message (Cc or Bcc). The addresses in the window's bottom-left box are drawn from your Address Book. When you click OK, the Send Mail window (bottom) comes up with information from the Email Recipients box of the Address Mail To… window.

Wherever you enter an address, you must click the appropriate radio button to indicate the status of the address for this message:

To	The direct recipient; if there are several recipients, enter each one separately.
Cc	An indirect recipient—someone you want to receive a copy of the message. To choose multiple Cc addresses, enter them separately. Your recipient(s) will know who received copies of the message.
Bcc	Blind carbon copy—someone you want to receive a copy of the message *without the direct recipient's knowledge*. To choose multiple Bcc addresses, enter them separately.

Click an address to select it, then click Use to move it into the Email Recipients box in the right side of the window, preceded by the word *To*, *Bcc*, or *Cc*—whichever radio button you selected.

Press ↵ or click OK to transfer addresses from the Email Recipients box, in order, into the Send Mail window (see Figure 2.3). Notice there are only two fields in Send Mail: To and Subject. Click the To... button to change the designation of addresses (from Cc to Bcc, say) or to enter new addresses. Click the drop-down list to *display* a Cc or Bcc address (if there is one) for this message.

To create your message, just type, as in any simple text editor. Don't be disappointed if you can't change your font type or size, or apply styles such as bold or italics. The recipient of your message wouldn't be aware of them anyway. However, you can copy (Ctrl+C), cut (Ctrl+X), and paste (Ctrl+V) text within a message.

Reformatting a Message

As you edit a news or mail message, your insertions and deletions may leave you with some lines too short and some too long, making your paragraphs look ragged. NetCruiser can help you tidy up your message before you send it.

To reformat, select lines of text and choose Edit ➤ Reformat Paragraphs. If no text is selected, Edit ➤ Reformat Paragraphs applies to the current paragraph. Each line will come as close to the right margin as possible.

You can automatically attach a signature file to your mail messages by creating a text file with your word processor called mail.sig, and placing it in the \netcom directory. Many people use "sig" files to attach mottos, bits of wisdom, phone numbers, shapes made at the keyboard, and other personal or business stuff to all their mail. Out of respect for recipients—and to reduce unnecessary Net traffic—it's a good idea to keep such files short (four lines or fewer).

When you're done, just click on Send. A Sending Mail icon appears in the lower left, then disappears when your message is on its way.

Messages you send are automatically saved in the \netcom\mail\outbox directory (which NetCruiser creates automatically during installation), with an eight-digit file name and extension of .msg (starting at 00000001.msg).

● Keeping an Address Book

With NetCruiser you don't have to remember the addresses of the many people you communicate with regularly. The Address Book does it for you. You get automatic access to your Address Book whenever you send mail or forward a mail message or news article. To add a bunch of names or prune the names you have, select Internet ➤ Address Book.

Adding an Individual Address At the Address Book window (Figure 2.4, top), click New Entry. The Edit Address Book Entry window comes up (Figure 2.4, middle). For each person you want to add, provide a full name (with spaces), an address, and, if you want, free-form comments. Click OK. Names entered here appear in the Address Mail To... window (when you send mail or forward mail or news), as well as in the Choose Entry From Address Book field of the Edit Email Group window. To change an address, select it in the Address Book, then click Edit. To delete an address, select it from the Address Book and click Delete.

Grouping Addresses You bring addresses together in a *group* because you routinely want to write to, or cc, the same group of people at the

Address Book

Address Book

New Entry

New Group

Edit

Delete

Done

Edit Address Book Entry

Name

Email Address

Comments

OK

Cancel

Edit Email Group

Group Name

Choose Entry From Address Book

Use ->

Email Addresses In Group

Delete

Comments

OK

Cancel

FIGURE 2.4: Use the Address Book (top) to keep track of both individuals you write to frequently (middle) and groups of people you write to at the same time (bottom). To edit data for either an individual or a group, select the name or group in the Address Book and click Edit.

same time. This is how you could communicate with everyone in your department at work, or with your softball team. At the Address Book window, click New Group. In the Edit Email Group window (Figure 2.4, bottom), first give the group a name. Then select and transfer (click Use) individual addresses from the Choose Entry From Address Book field to the Email Addresses in Group field. You can even include groups in larger groups, but in so doing you are transferring many *individuals* to the larger group, not really creating a group of groups. To edit a group, select the group in the Address Book, then click Edit. To delete a group (but not the individuals' addresses in the group), select it from the Address Book and click Delete.

● Finding a Mail Address

None of the common methods for finding a mail address is very good, not even the one that NetCruiser provides you, called *finger*. This is no fault of the tools, but a reflection of the absence of a central Internet directory, although researchers are working hard to devise a standard for collecting and disseminating "directory assistance" on the Internet. After all, there is not even a national *telephone* white pages in the U.S., and the global Internet consists of networks and computers, not individuals.

When in doubt, call. You have to tie up the phone line in any case, so what's the difference, and it's often faster.

Whois A *whois* database lists information about people and organizations. Searching such a database is easy using the Unix whois command. The largest (still proportionally very small) database of people throughout the Internet is at the InterNIC Registration Services Host, whose location is rs.internic.net; this service is available by telnet or gopher. This is a good way of finding a network administrator, not a network user.

If you're trying to find someone at a specific, usually large, university or organization, there's a chance the institution has its own gopher (you'll learn more about gopher in Chapter 6), and that a top-level gopher choice will be something like "campus-wide e-mail." Using gopher as a window onto a current campus whois database, you can often find the person you're seeking on a campus or large organization.

The Notre Dame gopher pulls together and provides a simple interface for Internet whois and other directories around the world, including Netfind. The gopher address is gopher.nd.edu and the path, once you're there, is Non-Notre Dame Information Sources ➤ Phone Books-Other Institutions. There are pointers to this site all over the Internet.

Let Finger Do the Walking

The charmingly named *finger* program checks whether someone is on a system without your having to send a message to that person.

To use finger you must first know the computer's name (like netcom.com) through which your friend gets access to the Internet. If the person has a login on that computer, and if that computer responds to finger commands, you might get back some valuable information about the user, at least an address.

To use NetCruiser finger, select Internet ➤ Finger, or click the button:

At the Site Chooser, enter the computer name where you want to look, or select one from a state's list. In the Finger dialog box that now comes up, enter all or part of the person's name. The output of the finger command is basic information about the person, plus the information contained in one or two optional files.

The real value of finger is not in its ability to track down people; its value here is usually minimal. Finger is more useful as a way of getting access to information that people want to share with the world. Information deliberately shared in this way ranges from the serious (getting up-to-date earthquake news or NASA newsfeeds about shuttle launches — see Figure 2.5) to the entertaining (getting the past week's TV Nielsen ratings) to the trivial (the inventories of Coke machines for certain college dorms). For some finger addresses and more pointers, look under *finger* in the NetCruiser Help system.

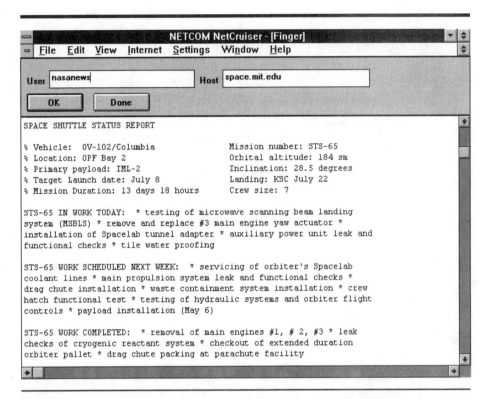

FIGURE 2.5: Finger has all sorts of uses—from finding the address of someone whose Net host you know, to taking the inventory of certain Coke machines, to learning about the up-to-the-moment doings of a NASA space shuttle.

Because finger has been abused by snoopy people in the past, some Internet computers do not support the command even when used by people on the same system. Usually, you will get a message if this is the case, but you may simply get no reply.

Using anonymous FTP (a tool covered in Chapter 5), you can receive an up-to-date reference on finding mailing addresses. To do so, use FTP to go to the MIT computer, pit-manager.mit.edu, then download the **finding-addresses** document from the /pub directory.

Communicating with People on Less Cool Networks

The Internet allows for communication with both research networks such as Usenet and BITNET and commercial networks such as CompuServe and America Online. More and more people use these commercial services as on-ramps onto the Internet, even though they get only a partial toolset and an indirect (not SLIP) connection. With NetCruiser you can exchange mail with people on the newer commercial systems.

In exchanging mail, it usually makes sense for one person to figure out how to reach the other, so the other person only has to reply to the message, which can usually be done by a mouse click or keystroke.

MCIMail To send mail to somebody with an account on MCIMail (a commercial e-mail service), add *@mcimail.com* to the end of their name or numerical address:

```
6646649@mcimail.com
```

or

```
jsixpack@mcimail.com
```

and put the result in the Address field. MCIMail will let you know if there are multiple jsixpack's and provide a listing to help you find the right one.

From MCI, someone reaches you on the Internet by typing at the To: prompt **[*your name*] (EMS)** and at the EMS prompt, **internet**, followed at the Mbx: prompt by your computer address (for example, **Netcom.com**).

CompuServe People on CompuServe have numeric addresses of the form *76543,210.* Note the number of digits (five and three) and the comma. To send a mail message to someone whose CompuServe address you know, just change the comma to a period, tack on *@compuserve.com,* and plug the result into the Address field of the NetCruiser mailer. For example,

```
12345.678@compuserve.com
```

Currently, CompuServe subscribers must pay to receive mail over the Internet.

For someone to send you a message from CompuServe, that person types **GO MAIL** (or makes the appropriate menu choices in WinCIM) and enters the following address in the address area:

```
>internet:username@computer.name
```

In other words, it's just like a message sent within the Internet, except for the addition up front of *>internet:.*

Other Commercial Online Services To send mail to a Delphi, Prodigy, or America Online user, the forms are *username@delphi.com, userID@prodigy.com,* and *username@aol.com.* Make sure to remove the spaces from the AOL user's name. As with CompuServe, Prodigy charges users for Internet e-mail. America Online users who want to send mail to you need only put your Net address in the To: field before composing a message.

This list is not comprehensive. Use FTP as explained in Chapter 5 to get more information: connect with the FTP computer at ra.msstate.edu, go to the directory pub/docs, and download the file called internetwork-mail-guide. **EFF's Guide to the Internet** also has good information as does NetCruiser's Help system.

● The Joys of Mailing Lists

E-mail is much like the mail service offered by the U.S Postal Service, except that it's faster, easier to manage, and you never leave home. In addition, mailing lists offer a way of communicating with many people at once. Unlike the unsolicited junk mail that your Post Office delivers, the electronic version of mail going from one person to many people is voluntary and solicited. Mailing lists are what draw many people to the Internet in the first place.

The Internet supports three ways of communicating with *groups* of people.

Non-automated Mailing Lists The smallest of the three types of group communication on the Internet, with their number running into the hundreds. These mailing lists are usually managed by a person, and are often moderated, which means that a real person reads and potentially filters out or edits messages. Any message you post to a list goes into the mailbox of every member.

Automated Mailing Lists An automated mailing list is managed by software, but its content is sometimes moderated by a person. Unlike non-automated mailing lists, these lists have a consistent interface, and offer you many options for customization. The most common automated lists are called *Listservs*, and usually run on BITNET's mainframe computers. You can join any of more than 4,000 Listserv lists. On Unix computers you're likely to encounter lists automated by programs called *listproc* or *majordomo*. The next sections focus on Listserv lists, the type of mailing list you're most likely to encounter. As with non-automated mailing lists, messages to a Listserv list go into the mailboxes of every member.

BITNET addresses are usually of the form AAAA@BBBBB. To send a message to a BITNET computer, you usually add **.bitnet** to the address. Increasingly you'll find Listserv software on computers on the Internet (not just BITNET), so the addresses will look more familiar.

Usenet Newsgroups There are more than 6,000 Usenet newsgroups, on every conceivable and numerous unprintable topics. Unlike Listservs and mailing lists, the newsgroups do not go into "subscribers'" mailboxes. They are for public consumption and must be downloaded from a server, such as Netcom's.

In terms of content, there's not much difference between mailing lists and Listservs, and between both and newsgroups; the mechanics of joining and using them are different, however—a legacy of the deliberate heterogeneity of the Internet as a network of networks. Also, many lists and newsgroups are "gatewayed"—made available in other forms, newsgroups as lists and so on.

Of the various types of lists, Usenet newsgroups offer the greatest number and richest variety of subjects covered, but until recently the worst interface to all that information. They are probably the most popular type of "list," yet mailing lists are still very popular today for many reasons:

◆ Some BITNET sites either do not have access to Usenet or give users access to only a handful of the 6,000-plus newsgroups; universities, for example, might screen out the "less serious" newsgroups.

Lists of Lists

Using anonymous FTP (see Chapter 5), start a session with rtfm.mit.edu (at MIT) and download the file /pub/usenet-by-group/news.answers/mail/mailing-lists/part*. This compilation contains the most active mailing lists. You can also get the latest version of this list from the Usenet news news.answers group.

Alternatively, you can get a list of Listserv lists by sending mail to List-serv@VM1.nodak.edu (that's a number *1* after *VM*); leave the subject blank and in the message type: **List Global.** To get a list of mailing lists about a specific subject send a mail message to listserv@bitnic.edu-com.edu, with your subject of interest in the Subject line (*English gardens*, say) and the following content (message): LIST GLOBAL/*text*. If your *text* is *English gardens*, you'll get a list of mailing lists relating to gardens. If you just put *LIST GLOBAL* in the message, you will get a long list of all Listserv mailing lists.

An excellent, up-to-date, and annotated source of information about both moderated mailing lists and unmoderated lists has been compiled by Stephanie Silva, and is available at Washington & Lee University's gopher, liberty.uc.wlu.edu. Several books purport to provide complete listings of mailing lists, but are necessarily incomplete and out of date. The Internet itself is usually the best source of information about the Internet.

◆ Moderated groups can restrict who can read or post to them, keeping out those who are disrespectful or abusive.

The rest of this chapter looks at mailing lists. Chapter 3 is devoted to the huge teeming topic of Usenet newsgroups.

Watch Your Manners

Lists differ, but no matter what list you join the following rules help keep the peace on the electronic frontier.

1. Stay in the wings for a while. Participation is a positive good on the Net, but read others' messages and get a sense of the culture of the group before taking part. It's OK to lurk, at first.

2. Remember that what you post to the list can be read by hundreds of people, of diverse background. Don't assume that everyone is interested in everything you say or will understand the way you say it. Keep in mind that not everyone will share your opinions. Think before you post.

3. Most lists have a separate address from the main address for requests asking to get on and off the list. Never send subscription or removal requests to the list itself if there is a different address for those requests. Such requests break down the continuity of discussions on the mailing lists and are annoying.

4. Send responses to questions posted on the list directly to the person who posted the question, not to the whole list. For example, if someone asks whether anyone has experience with a particular piece of hardware, 50 people might respond, and others on the list wouldn't want to see 50 responses of "I do."

5. When you do get interesting information via private e-mail in response to a question you asked in mailing list, be sure to summarize the answers and post them for the whole group to see. This prevents the same questions from coming up repeatedly.

Manually Maintained Mailing Lists

Most non-automated mailing lists are moderated or at least administered by a person. Once you know the name and address of the list you're interested in, you send a normal mail message to the moderator, usually by adding a –*request* to the list's name. How do you get a list of mailing lists? Check out the Lists of Lists sidebar for some guidance.

If you're interested in joining one of the Microsoft Access lists, ms-access@ eunet.co.at, you first send a message to the moderator, ms-access-request@ eunet.co.at. In the body of the message, request membership. It's also a good idea to request the address to which you can address all the members. In this case, you would send messages to all the list's members using the same address, but without the -*request*: ms-access@eunet.co.at.

Using a Listserv List

Listserv lists offer you a greater range of discussion groups to join and more options than mailing lists. Here are some topics to which Listservs are devoted:

Listserv	BITNET Address
Supercomputers in Central Europe	SCCE-L@PLTUMK11
Clock/Watch Repair, Collecting, and Construction	CLOCKS@SUVM
Electronic Music	EMUSIC-D@AUVM
Artificial Intelligence	IAMEX-L@TECMTYVM
Interactive Financial Planning System	IFPS-L@VTVM1
Distance Education	DED-L@UALTAVM
Backgammon Strategy	BKGAMMON@INDYCMS
Jane Austen	AUSTEN-L@MCGILL1
J.R.R. Tolkien	TOLKIEN@JHUVM
Tornado Warning Dissemination	WX-TOR@UIUCVMD

It's a good idea to get comfortable with the mechanics before getting caught up in the content.

Joining a List

When you find the name of a Listserv mailing list you want to be on, send a message to the Listserv *software*—not the list itself.

> You need to know **two** addresses for any list you're interested in, but they're easy to tell apart. Listserv@**computer.name** goes to the computer program that automates the list and handles your subscription request as well as your other interactions with the list. To post messages to the **people** on the list, you use **the name of the list@computer.name**. For example, you subscribe to the list devoted to the academic study of Buddhism at **Listserv@ulkyvm.louisville.edu**, but to reach all the members you post to **buddha-l@ulkyvm.louisville.edu**. Same computer, different recipients (one human, one not). If you address a subscription request to an actual list, your message will wind up in the mailboxes of perhaps hundreds of members—a bad way of introducing yourself.

The Listserv software ignores the subject of your subscription (or other house-keeping) message: it reads only the address and body. Enter the necessary Listserv commands in the body. Your message can have more than one Listserv command in it, as long as each command appears on a separate line.

For example, to join the mailing list on college hockey, you would send mail to Listserv@MAINE (a computer that might be handling many lists). The mail can have any subject (the program ignores that line), and the contents of the message would be a single line:

```
SUBSCRIBE HOCKEY-L Joseph Sterne
```

Instead of Joseph Sterne, you put in your real name.

When it gets a message, Listserv processes the commands and sends back a response. For instance, when you join a mailing list, Listserv sends back an acknowledgment and any introductory information about the mailing list. To confirm you're a member, send a message to Listserv@MAINE, or wherever, with CONFIRM HOCKEY in the body.

Listserv Options: Getting It Just Right

The Listserv program itself gives you many options that can simplify and customize the way the list works for you. Listserv can, if you know how to ask correctly, search through archived (old) messages for specific information, give you information about the membership list, stop messages from coming to you while you're on vacation, and more.

Don't forget to notify Listserv, not the list itself, of your preferences. In messages to a Listserv, it's okay to use lowercase.

Getting Help For starters, if you need help about the list in general, send Listserv a message with **HELP** in the body. You can also put **INFO** *topic* in the body, to receive information about a specific topic. The available topics are mostly technical. **INFO FAQ** will get the list server to send you a list of frequently asked questions (do this if you're new to lists!). **INFO FILEs** and **INFO DATABASE** are messages that tell the list server to inform you of any data it is storing in a database and of the ways you can get access to the database—a useful way of tracking down specific information contained in earlier messages.

FAQs (frequently asked questions) are an excellent source of information on the Internet. Keep an eye out for them. Many Usenet newsgroups (discussed in Chapter 3), especially news.answers, are good places to look for FAQs.

Getting Acknowledgment If you want acknowledgment—confirmation that a message you posted was received by the list—send Listserv a message with **SET** *listname* **ACK** in the body of the message. You'll get a copy of every message you post on the list. Unless you *SET ACK*, you won't be told whether your message was received (*NOACK*). Even if you do *SET ACK*, however, there's no way of knowing whether a message is actually read and by whom.

Temporarily Suspending Service If you want to stop mail from coming to your mailbox temporarily, send a message to Listserv with **SET** *listname* **MAIL POSTPONE** in the body. When you return, type **SET** *listname* **MAIL ACK**.

This option can come in handy if you will be away even a few days. Mail piles up fast if you subscribe to many lists.

Getting Digests of Listserv Messages If you don't want a hundred or a thousand messages a day, you can send a message to the Listserv at your list's computer with the following message in the body: **SET** *listname* **DIGEST**. The downside to digests is that it's hard to respond to an individual message in the digest, since the address of that message will differ from the address of the digest. A digest can come in handy if you've temporarily turned mail off.

Learning More about Others If you'd like a list of all members of the Listserv, send a message to Listserv with **RECIPIENT** *listname* in the body. If you want information about list members, send a message to the Listserv with **REVIEW** *listname* in the body. The computer sends you a list of members of the list, including the list header. You can add sorting options to the message, preceding each one by a left parenthesis, such as **(BY NAME**. Other useful options are **BY COUNTRY** (to sort by country of origin) and **BY USERID** (to sort by mail address). If you're just curious and want statistics about membership and usage for the list, send a message to Listserv with **STATS** *listname* in the body.

Reviewing Your Options To get information on your subscription options for a list, write a message to Listserv and put **QUERY** *listname* in the message. If you subscribe to many lists on the same computer, you can put an asterisk (*) instead of a specific list name to see options you've set for all the lists.

Unsubscribing from a List

Send a message to Listserv@*computer.name*, and in the body of the message put **SIGNOFF** *listname*. You can use an asterisk (*) instead of a list name to remove yourself from all lists on that server. You *must* unsubscribe from the same address you subscribed with.

Mail Secrets

The beauty of mail is its versatility. You can learn more about resources in your field, meet new people, retrieve files, do archie queries (more about this in Chapter 5, on FTP), and more.

Using Lists to Discover Internet Resources

Joining a list can introduce you to a wealth of Internet resources in your area of interest, especially information that's accessible using *other* tools.

Take for example the CoSN (Consortium for School Networking) list, which promotes the Internet as a teaching tool in the classroom and also lobbies for issues of importance to teachers in this field. CoSN-list members inform each other of new educational gophers, telnet sites, and World Wide Web "pages."

Real knowledge is exchanged as well on CoSN. Congressional deliberations and pronouncements from the Baby Bells about the future of schooling wind up in CoSN members' mailboxes sooner in some cases than they appear in the newspapers. CoSN subscribers keep each other abreast of conferences and training opportunities in the field of K–12 networking. The moderator, Gleason Sackman, posts messages from other lists of likely interest to CoSN members. And for people new to the field, CoSN is a way of learning the lay of the land: who are the experts, what are the issues, where are the jobs.

 If you're changing fields, a mailing list is an excellent way to learn about opportunities, but it is important to respect the line between issues of concern to all subscribers and issues of interest to an individual. Some lists do not wholeheartedly approve of individuals using the list to look for work. It's best to communicate about issues of personal concern directly with individual members of the list, rather than with everyone. And as always, it's best to lurk on a list to get a sense of its temper before raising any issue of strictly personal concern.

Getting Files by Mail

Mail also provides a fairly simple way of retrieving *files*. If you'd like official documents from the White House about healthcare, Bosnia, or NAFTA (the North American Free Trade Agreement), for example, you can send a mail message to the White House's mail server, publications@white-house.gov, with **topic *subject*** in the body of the file. You'll receive a list of numbered files.

To get a file on Bosnia, you reply with **sendfile *filenumber*** in the body. Figure 2.6 shows the results of one such request.

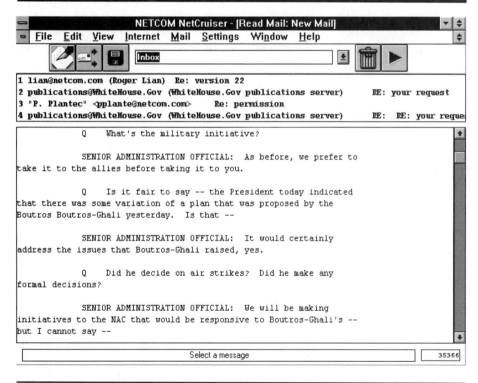

FIGURE 2.6: Official Washington is going online. After reading official statements such as this one (a White House briefing about the Gorazde crisis of 1994), you can take part in livelier and less official mailing lists and Usenet newsgroups.

Using Mail to do Archie Queries

A related example of the usefulness of mail is archie, the FTP utility that identifies FTP sites with files of interest to you. Because archie searches can take a long time online and the results can be voluminous, mail is an efficient way of doing an archie search and managing the results, if you aren't in a rush.

You'll learn more doing mail searches with archie in Chapter 5.

Mail and mailing lists are flexible tools, and you can take advantage of them in many ways in your daily life and work. Usenet news, which you'll learn about in the next chapter, is a little less personal, but it lets you take part in an even greater variety of online groups, with even greater ease.

Usenet News: 6000 Points of Light

After mail, Usenet is the Internet's most widely used tool, with around five million active readers in dozens of countries. That's about three times the circulation of *The Wall Street Journal*. Around 50,000 articles are posted to Usenet each day, generating about 100 MB of computer data a day.

You'll find Usenet newsgroups on music, movies, politics, language computers, computers, whatever. If you can think of it, it's being discussed. If you can make a living at it, it has a newsgroup. If it's about computers it has five newsgroups. And if it doesn't exist you can create it.

In the bad old days you had to struggle with a difficult-to-use Unix "news reader" called *rn*. Now NetCruiser gives you the tools you need to mingle in the virtual world with point-and-click simplicity. This chapter takes you on a tour of the Usenet frontier and introduces the NetCruiser tools for bringing some order to it.

What Is Usenet?

Usenet is both a physical network and a social one—the world's town square. As a physical network, Usenet is made up of computers that share *data*. The unit of data on Usenet is an *article*, and each article belongs to a *newsgroup*. Usenet's job is to see that articles originating on one computer are sent to every other computer in the network as quickly as possible. To accomplish this it uses a number of other networks, including the Internet. So porous is the wall between Internet and Usenet that you rarely realize they are separate networks.

As a social network, Usenet consists of thousands of electronic forums, or *newsgroups*, each devoted to a particular topic—from martial arts to mergers and acquisitions.

In a newsgroup people post *articles* (Figure 3.1). It's called an *article* because that is the standard unit of news—the kind you read in the newspaper and by extension, in Usenet news. Unlike mail, there is no privacy in a newsgroup. Anyone can join just about any newsgroup, and each message can be read by anyone.

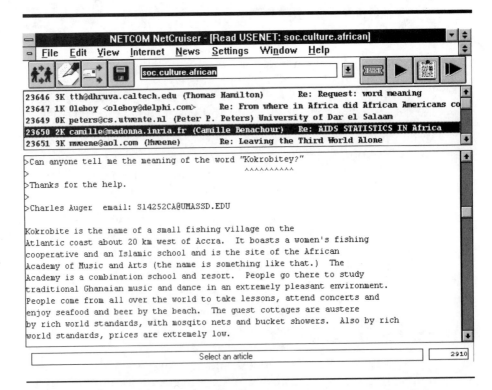

FIGURE 3.1: An article, the basic unit in a Usenet newsgroup — you can get the answer to any question on a USENET newsgroup.

Open forums with a huge audience cause ideas to spread quickly across Usenet. To communicate with people from every imaginable background, the denizens of Usenet have created a common frame of reference—a strange blend of openness and anonymity. There's even a newsgroup, alt.anonymous, devoted to anonymity.

Face to Face across the Net

Unlike mailing lists, most Usenet newsgroups are usually unmoderated; you have just as much say in what happens as anyone else. Distinctions of class, race, and sex have little impact, since all you know about someone is an Internet address. As the dog at the keyboard says, in the *New Yorker* cartoon, "the great thing about the Internet is no one knows you're a dog."

Chapter 2 discusses the difference between mailing lists and Usenet newsgroups.

A Taxonomy of Newsgroups

You cannot read more than a tiny fraction of the news, so you are going to have to be selective in choosing newsgroups. To choose a newsgroup in the first place, even using NetCruiser's simplified interface, you need to know a little about how newsgroups are named. Newsgroup names look like this:

soc.feminism

rec.music.classical

alt.2600

comp.os.linux.help

alt.asian-movies

news.answers

talk.abortion

Most newsgroup names are descriptive or self-explanatory, some are not, but all belong to a formal hierarchy. Look at these names:

> comp.os.linux.announce
>
> comp.sys.pc.hardware.cd-rom
>
> comp.sys.ibm.pc.soundcard
>
> comp.sys.next.announce
>
> comp.Unix.wizards

Each component of a newsgroup name—each level of the hierarchy—is separated by a period. From left to right names go from general to specific. The *first-level* component of all the newsgroup names above is *comp*, in this case the hierarchy dedicated to newsgroups about computers. *os*, *sys*, and *Unix* are the next level—the more specific subtopics under computers, standing for operating system, system, and Unix. comp.os.linux.announce is a newsgroup devoted to announcements about something very specific and of interest to a few Unix wizards, the linux operating system.

 Newsgroup names become increasingly arbitrary after the first level. You should get comfortable with all the first-level hierarchies, plus the lower-level categories for the subjects you're interested in.

Don't confuse the Internet's domain name system with Usenet's newsgroup-name hierarchy. They look alike but operate by a different scheme: *netcom.com* (domain name) is the name of a group of computers, but *netcom.netnews* (newsgroup name) is a sort of container for articles that will be distributed across *thousands of computers*. In domain names the most general domain is the *last* element of the name; in newsgroup names, the highest (most general) level of the hierarchy is the *first* element.

The Traditional Newsgroup Categories

The top-level categories correspond to certain broad classes of subject matter, as follows.

Comp This large hierarchy is devoted to the discussion of computer-related topics. Computers get a lot of coverage on Usenet. After all, everyone on Usenet must have at least some experience using computers. This is where to find information on specific operating systems and hardware. You'll find talk about more arcane computer science subjects such as artificial intelligence and computer graphics as well as business-oriented talk about databases and networks. This is the place to look for forums on software applications, such as the Access, FoxPro, and Paradox databases.

The comp hierarchy is about six times larger—has six times as many groups—as sci, the hierarchy devoted to all the sciences!

Misc These are the few newsgroups that don't really belong anywhere else. You can find good groups here devoted to taxes, children, writing, jobs, and items for sale.

News These are groups that pertain to Usenet itself. This is a great place to start your explorations of the news.

Don't confuse what's in the news hierarchy with **real** news, which you'll find under the Clarinet news service hierarchy, **Clari**.

Rec These groups are for the discussion of recreational activities: the arts, hobbies, movies, books, food, sports, and so on. This is a large hierarchy and you'll almost certainly find people discussing your favorite diversion here.

Sci This hierarchy contains newsgroups on various scientific fields of study, such as physics, math, anthropology, molecular biology, and psychology.

Soc These newsgroups are about social issues and different cultures. There are a number of soc.culture groups about specific cultures around the world, including the cultures of Afghanistan, Canada, Sri Lanka, and many other countries.

Talk These noisy newsgroups focus on highly controversial subjects; they in turn relieve the rest of Usenet of a lot of noise. Here you'll find discussions about gun control, religion, abortion rights, and politics of every stripe.

The Alternative Newsgroups

Another set of first-level hierarchies, the *alternative* newsgroup categories, have traditionally not had as wide a distribution, but the biggest are available using NetCruiser—alt, biz, and clari. There are fewer restrictions on the creation of new newsgroups in the alt hierarchy, so strange groups are created, and strange messages posted in the alternative hierarchy. Currently just over half the traffic on Usenet News is made up of articles belonging to alternative newsgroups.

Starting a newsgroup is a fairly formal process. For more information about the process, use anonymous FTP (which you'll learn about in Chapter 5), to go to rtfm.mit.edu. The file you want to read is called How_to_create_a_new_USENET_newsgroup, and its directory path is /pub/usenet-by-group/news.groups/. There is a huge amount of information about newsgroups in this directory.

Here are the largest alternative categories available to you using NetCruiser:

Alt Weird things. A huge category, for a good reason—there are no restrictions on newsgroup creation in the alt category; anyone can make a new newsgroup for any reason. Most of the new groups here fizzle out quickly, but this is also the place where you post and read articles about Elvis, Barney, and sex.

Biz A semi-commercial set of newsgroups, some of which are moderated. Turn here for information about computer vendors such as SCO, DEC, Zeos, and NeXT.

The posting of advertisements and commercial information has been traditionally frowned upon on Usenet, and many biz and clari newsgroups are moderated in order to keep the information content high and marketing noise low.

Clari *Real* news articles, often taken from commercial news services. *Most newsgroups here are moderated.* ClariNet newsgroup articles actually read like a newspaper. There are many groups in here covering world news, local news, technology issues, business news, sports, editorial columns, and whatever you might expect to find in a major paper (but not the comics or crosswords, at least yet). Netcom receives these groups by paying a fee to ClariNet, a private company.

 It's easy enough to **subscribe** to a moderated group—to read articles posted to it. The articles you **post** to the group, however, are subject to being read, edited, or filtered out.

Gnu Articles pertaining to the Free Software Foundation (FSF). One of the goals of the FSF is to create a new advanced operating system with free source code.

K12 Devoted to educational issues for grades K–12. There are newsgroups for conversations among students, teachers, and classrooms across the world. Teachers, in particular, take part in newsgroups organized by the core subjects of the curriculum.

Regional Newsgroups

In addition to the big hierarchies with worldwide distribution and the alt hierarchies with spottier distribution, you'll encounter regional groups, which carry articles of concern primarily to certain localities. Because Netcom has access sites all over the United States, NetCruiser makes available some of these regional groups. Here are some examples of regional groups.

First-level Regional Newsgroups	Applies to What Area
ba	The San Francisco Bay area
la	Los Angeles
pdx	Portland, Oregon
dc	Washington, D.C.

There is also a *Netcom* category—newsgroups that tell you what's going on at Netcom and on the Internet, and give you an opportunity to communicate about the company.

The Problem with Newsgroup Names

It started out pretty well with the seven traditional groups, which had more or less well-demarcated areas of coverage. The comp groups are still the best place to look for computer information, and the rec groups are still the best place to look for people talking about the arts. But with the addition of the alt groups and the regional groups, however, the whole hierarchical naming scheme has lost some of its utility. Newsgroups about music can wind up in the rec or alt groups, or elsewhere, and computer information can wind up under biz or alt, as well as under comp. NetCruiser, you'll see, has a good answer to this problem—a subject-oriented organization of newsgroups that cuts across the hierarchies.

NetCruising on Usenet

The NetCruiser newsreader allows you to quickly and easily find the newsgroups you are looking for, subscribe to them, then read and respond to any articles that interest you. In organizing groups by subject, NetCruiser has overcome many of the limitations of the hierarchical naming scheme.

Subscribing and Unsubscribing to Newsgroups

To read a newsgroup with the newsreader, you must first subscribe to it. Don't be mislead by the word *subscription*: The process isn't as time-consuming as subscribing to a magazine or as formal as joining a mailing list, and there are no strings attached; you can "unsubscribe" at any time by clicking a button.

NetCruiser divides newsgroups into more or less logical groupings by *subject*.

Use both NetCruiser's categories and the hierarchical system to locate newsgroups. That is, within NetCruiser's categories you can search for more or less credible (clarinet) or interesting (rec) or controversial (alt) or technical (comp) newsgroups.

To subscribe to a newsgroup, select Internet ➤ Choose Usenet Newsgroup to bring up the Select Usenet Newsgroups window (Figure 3.2). Newsgroup Categories (subjects) are in the upper pane of the window; subscription lists in the lower pane, the Newsgroup Mover.

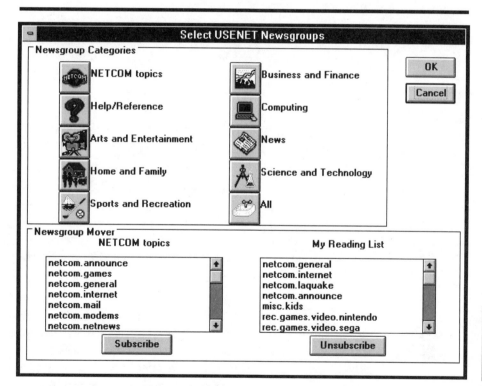

FIGURE 3.2: At the Select Usenet Newsgroups window, you choose the newsgroups you want to see and drop the ones you don't like.

Most Newsgroup categories in the window consist of *several* first-level hierarchies:

Newsgroup Category in NetCruiser	First-level Hierarchy
Netcom Topics	netcom
Help/Reference	alt, ca, comp, news, sci, soc, talk
Arts and Entertainment	alt, rec
Home and Family	alt, misc
Sports and Recreation	alt, clari (sports news), rec
Business and Finance	alt, biz, clari
Computing	comp, gnu
News	clari
Science and Technology	sci
All	all first-level hierarchies

You select a newsgroup category by clicking on one of the Newsgroup Category buttons in the top pane, or you can just click on the All button if you want to view all the newsgroups Netcom carries.

The bottom pane, the Newsgroup Mover, is where you actually subscribe to, and unsubscribe from, newsgroups. When you select a category in the top of the window, all the newsgroups in that category are listed in the left-hand box in the lower half of the window, called *Category* topics, with *Category* replaced by the name of the button you clicked in the Newsgroup Categories pane, such as *Netcom*.

 In the topic list in the Newsgroup Menu, click on and drag the scroll bar's **elevator box** (the little box that shows you where you are relative to the beginning and end of a document) to zip through the newsgroups in the category you selected; there can be hundreds of newsgroups in a category.

When you find a newsgroup that sounds interesting, simply select its name (click on it), then click on the Subscribe button. The newsgroup is added to My Reading List, showing all the newsgroups to which you subscribe, from all categories. To read articles for the newsgroup you just subscribed to, first click OK to finish subscribing. That's all it takes to subscribe to a newsgroup.

You can subscribe to a newsgroup while using the Read Usenet window. (That's the window where you'll do most of your work and play with Usenet. See "Working with Newsgroups.") From the News menu, choose Select Newsgroup. The Select Usenet Newsgroups dialog box comes up, from which you make selections as described in the previous sections. With the Read Usenet window open and nothing selected, you can also visit a newsgroup by simply typing its name in the drop-down box in the toolbar. To subscribe to a newsgroup you are visiting, click the Subscribe button.

Unsubscribing

To unsubscribe from a newsgroup, you just reverse the procedure of the previous sections. In the Select Usenet Newsgroup window, use the scroll bar's elevator box for My Reading List to locate the group you don't want to read anymore. Select it, then click on Unsubscribe. It disappears from the list.

Subscribe to the netcom.test newsgroup if you want some practice subscribing and unsubscribing to newsgroups, as well as posting and reading articles. You will find this newsgroup in the Netcom category. There is also a misc.test newsgroup that serves the same purpose.

If you have subscribed to a newsgroup and find you don't like it, you can also unsubscribe from the Read Usenet window by selecting the newsgroup and clicking the Unsubscribe button.

Working with Newsgroups

To read articles in a newsgroup, select Internet ➤ Read a USENET news-group or click on the button:

From the Select a Newsgroup window, double-click on one of the news-groups you've subscribed to (see Figure 3.3).

After you select a newsgroup, the Retrieve Article Headers window comes up for that newsgroup (Figure 3.3), showing you the numbers of the old-est available article (top field) and the most recent article (bottom field).

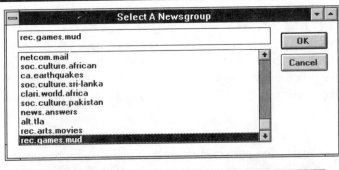

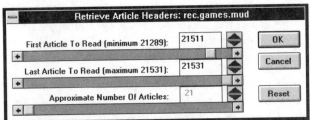

FIGURE 3.3: The Select a Newsgroup window (top) shows you the newsgroups you have subscribed to, in the order you selected them. Use a newsgroup by double-clicking its name. The Retrieve Article Headers window (bottom) comes up automatically. Tell NetCruiser how many articles you want to read. You can scroll up from the lowest article number available or down from the highest. Reset the numbers if you forget the range.

NetCruiser defines the First Article to Read as the last article you read during your last session. It defines the Last Article to Read as the most current one available. You can't see articles before the First Article to Read.

Click on the appropriate up and down arrows or use the horizontal scroll bar to select a manageable range of articles. To restore the minimum and maximum numbers you started with, press Reset. Click OK to accept a range.

The status bar displays a message, *getting headers*, and shows you the number range of the headers being downloaded. (It's more efficient to download headers than entire articles.) When NetCruiser finishes, it displays headers in alphabetical order by subject, in the header pane. To see articles in a different order, choose View ➤ Sort By ➤ Article Number or View ➤ Sort By ➤ Sender, then re-select the newsgroup.

Selecting an Article to Read

The header list allows you to quickly browse the subject lines of all unread articles, so you can choose and read the likely looking ones. Some of the articles in Figure 3.4 have *Re:* in the subject line. This means that the article is a response to a previous posting.

Reading and Responding to Articles

To open an article to read, double-click on it. The large lower pane displaying the full text of an article appears when you select its header. The Read Usenet window has its own toolbar at the top and a message (status) bar at the bottom.

 Maximize the Read Usenet window (click on the upward-pointing arrow) in the upper right of the window. Resize the header and message panes to increase the amount of message you can see at a time.

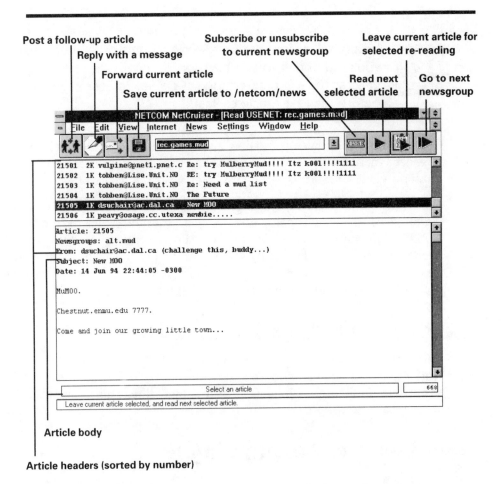

Post a follow-up article

Reply with a message

Forward current article

Save current article to /netcom/news

Subscribe or unsubscribe to current newsgroup

Read next selected article

Leave current article for selected re-reading

Go to next newsgroup

Article body

Article headers (sorted by number)

FIGURE 3.4: The header list gives you an overview of the articles waiting for your attention. In the articles **you** post, make subject lines as descriptive as possible. [Re] identifies articles that are responses to other articles—forming **threads**.

How It Works

Usenet articles are transported between computers called *NNTP* servers. (NNTP stands for Network News Transfer Protocol, a standard for exchanging Usenet news over the high-speed network connections allowed by the Internet.) When you subscribe to a newsgroup, your reader connects to an NNTP server at Netcom. The first thing you can see it do is retrieve the headers of the articles in the group so it can show you the subject lines. When you click on an article's subject, the NetCruiser reader requests the article itself from the NNTP server and displays it on your screen.

When you post an article, the process is reversed. NetCruiser on your computer connects to Netcom's NNTP server and sends your article, which gets in line with other articles, and is sent off to other servers. This is how your message wends its way through the Usenet, traveling across the network in only a few hours. (The largest Usenet sites may get your article in just a few minutes, but it may take several days for the article to filter down to smaller sites.)

The eight toolbar buttons correspond to various posting and news-navigation functions. Buttons simplify the task of managing articles and responding to them.

To post a **follow-up** article to the current article *to subscribers*.

To **reply** to the currently displayed article *via mail*—just like replying to a mail message. The Send Mail window appears (described in Chapter 2). When you choose Reply, you are first asked whether to "quote" the original article in your response. The reply is automatically addressed to the article's author, and the subject line is picked up from the original posting (see Figure 3.5). Simply type your response into the text box and click on the Send button (or Cancel if you change your mind). The Sending Message [Send Mail] icon appears for a moment as the article is sent to Netcom's mail server.

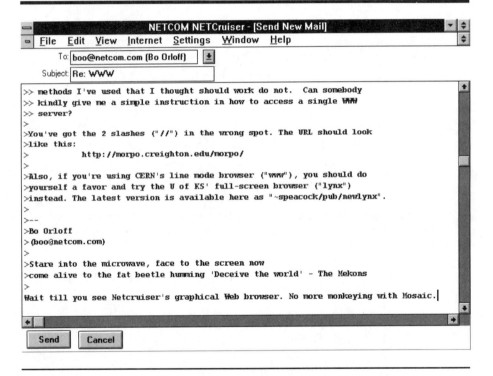

FIGURE 3.5: You use the Send Mail screen when you want to reply directly to someone who has posted a Usenet article. This particular message is going to the person who replied to someone else's question about the World Wide Web. That person wouldn't know of this mail message unless you posted a follow-up message to the newsgroup.

Forwarding an article allows you to *mail* an article to someone else who might find it interesting. Its function is similar to the Forward function in mail. When you click the Forward button the Send Mail window appears, with the original message "quoted." Simply put in the address of the person you want to send the article to in the To: text box, and maybe edit or add a comment or two to the body of the message, then click on Send. There's an art to "quoting" or "summarizing" just the part of the article you are responding to. When you forward an article, you bring up NetCruiser's Address Mail To... window. The window is described in the "Sending Messages" section of Chapter 2.

Saves the article to \netcom\news, which NetCruiser creates during installation.

A fast way to **subscribe** to or **unsubscribe** from a newsgroup. Just select the newsgroup and click the button to remove it.

Read the **next selected article**.

Leave Selected, Read Next—leave the current article *selected* so you can re-read it later in your Usenet session, and read the next selected article. See "Reading Selected Articles."

Get and display the headers of the **next newsgroup,** from the newsgroups you see in the drop-down list. Newsgroups are listed there in the order you chose them, not in alphabetical order.

Printing To print an article, select File ➤ Print Article.

Reading Selected Articles

After the article headers are downloaded, you can double-click an interesting-looking header if you want to read just that one article, or you can select a group of headers to read all the associated articles. You can select a group of headers with the keyboard or mouse, using Shift (for continuous headers) or Ctrl (for discontinuous ones). To start reading articles, click the Read Next Selected Article button. After you've finished reading an article, you can either

◆ Click the Read Next Selected Article button again to go to the next article and *de-select the current article*.

◆ Click the Leave Selected, Read Next button if you want to read the next selected article and *leave the current article selected* for re-reading later, and go on to the next selected article.

If you leave articles selected, NetCruiser will automatically re-display them when you click one of the Read Next buttons after you've gone through all the articles you had originally selected.

Leave articles selected when you think you might want to reply to an article, but you first want to read what has been said in later articles.

Posting a New Article

To post a new article to a newsgroup, choose Internet ➤ Post to USENET-Out or click on the Post-to-Usenet button on the toolbar.

The Post to Usenet window appears (see Figure 3.6). Because much of your communication with people in the group takes place while you're using the Read window, you'd use the Post window to send something new to the group.

First type in the name of the news group where you want the new article to appear in the Newsgroups box.

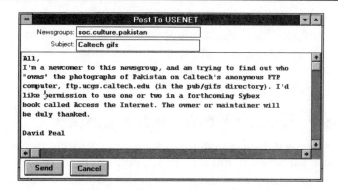

FIGURE 3.6: You use the Post to Usenet window if you are not responding to another article, that is, you want to start a new subject in a newsgroup.

To cross-post (send an article to more than one newsgroup), separate the multiple newsgroup names by commas.

In the Subject box type in the subject line of the article. This is the line that will appear in the header list of the newsreader screen. Try to make the subject line as descriptive as possible.

Now just enter the text of your message in the message box. You can use standard Windows cut-and-paste techniques to import text from other applications, but don't bother trying to import graphic or other non-text items. You can't do it in NetCruiser, but the recipient probably couldn't read it anyway.

 You can automatically attach a **signature file** to your news articles by creating a text file with your word processor called news.sig, and placing it in the \netcom directory. With a news.sig, as with a mail.sig, you can attach bits of wisdom, phone numbers, and other information to anything you send to other people. Out of respect for recipients, it's a good idea to keep your sigs under four lines.

When you're done, click on the Send button. The Send Message icon appears, and reports on the status of your message until it has been received at Netcom's computer, and sent hence to the world. It may still take a few minutes before your message actually appears in the destination newsgroup or newsgroups. If you don't want to send your message, press Cancel.

The Politics of Posting: Flaming

Flame wars—shouting matches—are a familiar ritual in newsgroups. Opinions can run to extremes on Usenet, perhaps because it can be difficult to express in writing the nuances that would be clear in speaking; perhaps because the anonymity of the Net relieves some people of the respect and tolerance they'd normally feel; perhaps because Usenet brings together such an incredible diversity of people; and hey, because it's fun. Whatever the reason, feelings can run high on Usenet.

If you like flame wars, there are several alternative (alt) news-groups devoted to flaming in general and even to abusing specific people and institutions.

The Politics of Posting: Emoticons

Emoticons were devised to diminish the online misunderstandings that other-wise result in flame wars. You can use these keyboard characters to represent your *real* intentions in your postings. With emoticons you can express a grin, a smile, a frown, a grimace, and hundreds of other emotions.

Emoticons

Misunderstandings are rife on the Usenet, so people have developed a way of signaling their emotions and intentions, called *emoticons* or *smileys*. Your basic smiley looks like this:

:-)

(Tilt your head to the left as you look at it.) The idea is it's supposed to look like a smiling person. Smileys are now ubiquitous, even on other net-works. Dozens of emoticons express other subtleties of meaning, but only a few are widely understood.

:-(	A frowning face; the writer is displeased
:-O	A surprised or shocked face
:-|	An unimpressed face
;-)	A wink

Places to Go, Things to Read

There is such abundance of information available on Usenet that it might seem a little arrogant to recommend newsgroups. But here are a few newsgroups where every new Usenet reader can profitably begin to explore. This small sampler is complemented by a larger listing of interesting and weird newsgroups in Table 3.1.

TABLE 3.1: Noteworthy Usenet Newsgroups

NEWSGROUP	WHY IT'S NOTEWORTHY
alt.activism	A strange mix of leftist and rightist politics. Political opposites square off here and, predictably, a lot of heat is generated.
alt.angst	Bitching, moaning, and whining.
alt.bbs.internet	Most of the discussion in this group is how to *get* internet access, and how to get bulletin board systems connected to the Internet. But there are also pointers to bulletin boards already on the Internet, and how to access them.
alt.censorship	Censorship is a subject that gets a lot of bandwidth on Usenet, much of it in this group. Controversy can run pretty high here, but it's an interesting subject with important Net ramifications.
alt.conspiracy	A bizarre mix of Chomskian political theory, UFOs, and anti-Semitism, this newsgroup runs the gamut from the banal to the appalling. Something here to offend everyone.

TABLE 3.1: Noteworthy Usenet Newsgroups (continued)

NEWSGROUP	WHY IT'S NOTEWORTHY
alt.current-events.*	These groups appear and disappear in response to recent news events.
alt.dcom.telecom	Discussion of the phone company, and telephony in general.
alt.discordia	Visit this group to see an inside joke taken way too far. And don't miss alt.illuminati. Don't these people have something better to do?
alt.dreams	People post and discuss their dreams here.
alt.drugs.caffeine	Coffee worship.
alt.en-sign.wesley.die.die.die	Just what it sounds like. Wesley Crusher haters meet here. Rumor has it that Will Wheaton himself reads this group from time to time.
alt.etc.passwd	No one posts here, but the concept is great. /etc/passwd is the file on Unix systems that contains (sometimes) encrypted passwords. There are programs available that will find weak passwords from these lists. I guess you are supposed to post passwd files here for cracking.
alt.fan.*	The alt.fan.* groups are pretty self-explanatory. Here you'll find the infamous pure-noise group alt.fan.rush-limbaugh. This is where you'll find alt.fan.shostakovich.
alt.feminism	This is the unmoderated sister group to soc.feminism. Look here for a lot of very smart women and a few very dumb men.

TABLE 3.1: Noteworthy Usenet Newsgroups (continued)

NEWSGROUP	WHY IT'S NOTEWORTHY
alt.flame	If you just can't get enough of flame wars, look in the alt.flame groups. Actually flame wars are even *less* interesting when you look at them out of context. Enjoy.
alt.horror	This group is mostly about the horror genre in books and movies, but you'll also find some discussion on the topic of scariness.
alt.journalism	Discussions on journalism, criticism of journalism, discussions about criticism of journalism, Criticism of discussions of journalism...
alt.paranet.*	The alt.paranet.* groups discuss paranormal phenomena of all sorts. 'alt.paranet.abduct'; you get the idea. Considering all the weird people on Usenet, these groups get amazingly little traffic.
alt.personals	Self-explanatory. Heavy traffic newsgroup. Did I mention that most Usenet readers are male? Did someone tell these people?
alt.politics.*	About what you'd expect. Lot's of noise.
alt.privacy	Discusses the issues of privacy, anonymity, and security on the net. Some interesting information here.

TABLE 3.1:   Noteworthy Usenet Newsgroups (continued)

NEWSGROUP	WHY IT'S NOTEWORTHY
alt.tv.*	Talk to people about staring at a video screen for hours while staring at a video screen for hours. If you want to see a joke taken way to far check out 'alt.tv.dinosaur.barney.die.die.die'. How long can it be before we get 'alt.tv.(dinosaur.barney.die.die.die).die.die.die'?
biz.jobs.offered	Electronic job listings. Be sure to check regional newsgroups for *.jobs.* groups too.
cern.skiclub	The cool place to be for physicist skiers, and would-be physicist skiers.
clari.biz.market	Commercial news articles on market trends and events. Daily quotes can be found in the sub-groups.
clari.news.top	Just what it sounds like. An arbitrary selection of the top news stories. Look out USA Today.
comp.ai.fuzzy	If you have to ask, don't bother.
comp.sys.ibm.pc.*	Since I know you're using one of these, I thought I would point you towards the PC and compatibles groups.
misc.activism.progressive	Good group. Mainly because it's moderated. Lots of information and no noise.
misc.consumers	Talk and advice on consuming. Here you can find information on buying a car or a home. Pretty good group.
misc.forsale	There are many newsgroups that offer things for sale, on Usenet, most of them regional or by item (computers, cars, etc.).

TABLE 3.1: Noteworthy Usenet Newsgroups (continued)

NEWSGROUP	WHY IT'S NOTEWORTHY
misc.invest	Another pretty good group if you need information about life insurance, mutual funds, the stock market, and so on.
rec.aquaria	Fish.
rec.arts.anime	A surprisingly high traffic group discussing Japanese animation. It's an interesting comment on Usenet demographics.
rec.arts.bodyart	Tatooing and body piercing are the topics on this ultra-hip newsgroup. The FAQs are impressive. Not that you really want to know this stuff.
rec.arts.fine	A quiet group. Here you'll find discussions about art theory, and about media and techniques.
rec.arts.poems	Many original works are posted here for discussion. It's a pretty harmonious group normally, but don't post if you are thin skinned, as some of the criticism can be heavy handed.
rec.humor.oracle	An interesting internet institution. Questions submitted to the Oracle are sent out to be answered by random netters, hopefully with some humor. The often funny results are posted here.
rec.kites	Someone I know likes kites, so I thought I'd put this here. Information on building, flying and fighting kites.
rec.music.*	There are a lot of rec.music groups, covering all types of music, for both musicians and listeners.

TABLE 3.1: Noteworthy Usenet Newsgroups (continued)

NEWSGROUP	WHY IT'S NOTEWORTHY
rec.org.mensa; rec.org.mensa.flame. flame.flame	The pretentious and the resentful hang out in these two groups respectively. Actually, everyone just hangs out in the first group, but I like the fact that the second group exists.
rec.pets.cats, rec.pets.dogs	The dog group gets about twice as much traffic as the cat group; you draw the conclusion.
rec.photo	High volume, lot's of information, and almost no noise make this a great newsgroup for discussion of photography equipment and techniques.
rec.skate	Inline skating, roller skating, and ice skating are discussed here. But the young and extremely cool hang out on alt.skate-boarding, thank god.
soc.motss	Considering its controversial content, this group for members of the same sex is surprisingly calm.

As you'd expect, there are clever online ways of getting lists of Usenet newsgroups. Check out the news.list newsgroup, where a master list of newsgroups is occasionally posted. Or, use anonymous FTP to download a list from rtfm.mit.edu. The directory is /pub/usenet-by-group/news.answers/active-news-groups. **Part1** and **part2** are the file names.

Getting Started on Usenet

The first place to look when you start reading Usenet is in the news hierarchy, which is devoted to Usenet goings on. These groups deal specifically with Usenet, and it's here you can find the answers you need to get your bearings.

Emily Post Is Lurking Out There

Usenet works only because users are willing to use it responsibly. You will hear much discussion about *netiquette* online. Here are some guidelines:

1. When you use Usenet, treat people with respect and courtesy. There is something about communicating through a computer screen instead of face to face that makes some people forget common courtesy. This makes Usenet a volatile place where much of the news is taken up by angry and abusive exchanges, or flame wars. If you witness a heated exchange, just stay out of it.

2. Keep in mind the broad audience that your articles can reach, and the different perspectives your readers might have on your ideas. Ideas that are unquestionable to you might be offensive to others.

3. Remember that no one can see you smile on the Usenet. Humor and sarcasm are much more difficult to express when writing than when speaking, so it's very easy for your humor to be misinterpreted. Remember, even if your humor is obvious to 99% of the people who read your message, that still leaves a potential 50,000 people who won't get the joke. And don't think that a simple explanation will ever mend hurt feelings. The offended reader will almost certainly respond with a nasty article, then a reader who got the joke will post about how stupid the first reader was, and away we go. A dry sense of humor can be quite a liability on Usenet, and irony is next to impossible. (See the Sidebar on Emoticons earlier in this chapter.)

4. Don't be offended by other peoples' ideas. Usenet really does require an open and forgiving attitude from readers. A lot of the flaming on the Net is the result of misinterpretation, rather than disagreement. And even if you do read something that you find truly offensive please do your best to ignore it. You will sometimes find people posting offensive or controversial positions just to get a rise out of other readers. This is called flame-bait. Please resist the temptation to respond to outrageous articles.

5. Every article you post to Usenet is data that is going to be transmitted to and stored on thousands of computers all over the world. The Internet isn't free, and neither is hard disk space.

6. Try to find the information you want before you request it. Take some time to read a newsgroup before posting to it. Newsgroup names don't always give you a good understanding of what a group is about. Many newsgroups have lists of frequently asked questions, or FAQs, intended to cut down on endlessly repeated questions that occur as people first start reading a new group. These FAQs are posted periodically, and make up some of the most useful reading you can do on Usenet. If you haven't been following the group and you have a question, always check the FAQ. You can find out about the location of FAQs in the news.answers group.

7. Try to keep your articles as short, clear, and concise as possible. This will make for efficient use of Usenet resources. It will also make you article easier to read, and more likely to generate useful responses. Always use clearly worded informative subject headers. Few people are going to read your article if it has a vague or incomprehensible header. If you are asking a question say so in the header. One common Usenet practice is to put a bracketed *[Q]* as the first thing in your header when you ask a question. You'll find you get more useful responses this way.

8. Post to the correct newsgroup, and don't cross-post unnecessarily. An article posted to the wrong newsgroup is a wasted article. No one is going to respond to it, and worse, twenty people are going to post about how lame it was to post that article here blah blah blah. And the mail you'll get—more wasted bandwidth. Cross-posting your article to different newsgroups is another risky undertaking. When posting follow-up articles, remember that if the original article was cross-posted to many newsgroups your response will, by default, also be posted to all those newsgroups. One of the most sadly humorous sights on Usenet is one person cross-posting to several newsgroups, and then ten self-appointed net-cops posting follow-ups about how irresponsible it was, and all *those* articles are automatically cross-posted to each newsgroup.

9. Read all the responses to a message before you post your own response, otherwise you risk duplicating someone else's response and looking silly. Articles don't arrive at every site in the same order, so sometimes this is unavoidable, but do your best. Also, summarize the original post in your response so that people don't have to go searching for the original article to understand your brilliant comments. NetCruiser has the ability to quote from the original article when you're posting a follow-up. Read some news and you'll see what I mean.

10. If a question is highly specific, and you don't think a lot of other people will want to hear the answer, send your response via mail rather than posting an article that will be distributed around the world. In fact sending responses via mail is never a bad idea. Often people who post questions will specifically request this, and will offer to summarize the mail responses in a new article for everyone to read. (Use NetCruiser's Reply function to do this.)

Now Hear This: news.announce.newusers This group carries periodic postings of articles written to help new Usenet users. Newsgroup lists, moderator lists, and numerous how-to articles are posted here. This is an excellent place to gather more information in preparation for blazing your own path. This *moderated* group is used only for the posting of informative articles.

Starting Out: news.newusers.questions This is a fairly heavily trafficked newsgroup where you will find helpful and knowledgeable people who can answer your Usenet questions. Don't be shy about posting here. Reading this group is a great way to get an understanding for the way Usenet works, and one of the best ways to use the news responsibly.

A Practice Run: netcom.test There are a number of test newsgroups on Usenet. Test groups are just what the name says, the newsgroups where you post test articles to figure out how your newsreader works. You can try posting follow-up articles to get the hang of summarizing.

Attention! netcom.announce Netcom events come to light here. Learn of major projects and appointments, find out what's going on at your favorite access provider. This is the company's way of speaking to you. You can communicate with netcom using technical support and e-mail, and by taking part in netcom.general.

Information Please: news.answers One of the best groups on Usenet. Periodical informative postings and FAQs from all the newsgroups on Usenet are cross-posted to here. Remember, FAQs are compilations of the questions most frequently asked in various newsgroups, but they can be much more than that. FAQs are often well-written introductions to newsgroup subjects, sometimes whole branches of science or art.

Remarkable intelligence and knowledge goes into many FAQs. If you receive only one newsgroup on Usenet, consider this one. The anonymous FTP site rtfm.mit.edu is one of several sites with FAQ archives.

Usenet Summits and Dives

Here are a few newsgroups where you might want to continue your explorations.

Life in the Big City Alt.folklore.urban gets a great deal of traffic. It is devoted to discussing, debunking, and celebrating modern legends and folklore (see Figure 3.7). There are actually several alt.folklore groups, on topics such as ghost stories and Coca-Cola. All are worth checking out, but AFU is the largest and arguably the best.

Internet Insider alt.internet.services discusses all kinds of Internet issues, including how to get access from remote places, the types of services available on the Internet, political issues affecting the Internet, and so on. Its subject matter is broader than its name might imply—which is true of most newsgroups (see Figure 3.8).

Internet-related groups appear under both the alternative (alt) hierarchy and the mainstream (comp) hierarchy.

```
>Oprah's name was mispelled on her birth certificate. She was to have been
>named "Orpah", which supposedly is from the Bible.

From the Bible Gateway on the WWW [http://unicks.calvin.edu/cgi-bin/bible]

Ruth 1:4
--------
And they took them wives of the women of Moab; the name of the one was
Orpah, and the name of the other Ruth: and they dwelled there about ten
years.

Ruth 1:14
---------
And they lifted up their voice, and wept again: and Orpah kissed her mother
in law; but Ruth clave unto her.

- Stephen "occasional AFU lurker"
```

FIGURE 3.7: An article from the alt.folklore.urban newsgroup. In Chapter 7 you'll learn to access pages on WWW (World Wide Web).

```
Newsgroups: alt.internet.services
From: barmiyan@wam.umd.edu (Amy Rebecca Ewing)
Subject: Are you addicted to the Internet?
Date: 18 Mar 1994 16:40:51 GMT

Hi! I am a freelance writer working on a story about internet addiction.
I'd appreciate any input on the following:

Are you an internet addict? Do you know someone who is? How has the
internet affected your work or social life? At what hours or for
how many hours a day are you logged on? What do you spend the most
time on?

I'd appreciate answers to these questions and any other facts you
could provide. Please e-mail responses!
```

FIGURE 3.8: This journalist knew where to go to find inquisitive Internauts. Next is a 12-step program for information junkies.

Puzzles Rec.puzzles covers all kinds of puzzles and logic problems. There is a periodic posting in this group of an immense list of puzzles. One of Usenet's best.

Politics The talk.politics.* newsgroups, where the * stands for *china, guns, mideast, soviet,* and others, are high-traffic, high-energy newsgroups. It's worth checking out just to see what big controversial newsgroups are like.

Movies Rec.arts.movies is a high-traffic group discussing—movies. Not a bad place to get the scoop on new films (see Figure 3.9). You can also check out rec.arts.movies.reviews for more formal commentary. For a different slant, drop by alt.cult-movies. The amount of information these people have on *Blade Runner* is a little scary. Get a life guys.

Wired Magazine The trendy newsgroup, alt.wired, has loose connections to the trendy magazine, *Wired*, and is the hangout of real and would-be cyberpunks and internauts.

The magazine Wired itself is available online using the World Wide Web. You'll learn how to get access to it in Chapter 7.

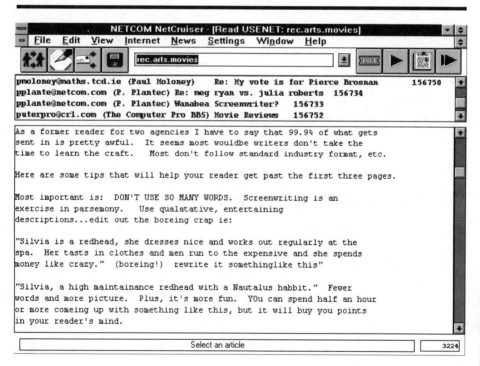

FIGURE 3.9: Helpful advice in the rec.arts.movies newsgroup.

Eating The several rec.food.* groups exchange thoughts about food as well as recipes (see Figure 3.10). These groups get a moderate amount of traffic, and contain little pure noise. They're a welcome respite from the more chaotic discussion newsgroups. The star (*) stands for type of recipe: from *drink* to *sourdough* to *veg*.

```
Article: 2258
Newsgroups: rec.food.sourdough
From: rroeder@infoserv.utdallas.edu
Subject: NEWBIE
Date: 12 Mar 1994 14:52:03 -0600

I'm new to made-at-home sourdough breads, in that I've never made any.
Where could I typically get "starter(s)", or do I get yeast and grow 'em
myself ?  Where can I get BASIC BASIC BASIC this-is-how-you-do-it-by-kneading
-the-dough instructions on how to make sourdough breads ?  I don't have a
"bread-making" machine.

Any and all help will be appreciated.

TIA !!
```

FIGURE 3.10: A newbie query to the sourdough forum. TIA is a TLA (three-letter acronym) for Thanks in Advance. TLAs are part of the Internet culture. So is helpfulness to newcomers.

The Pleasures of Usenet

No matter what you want to do or know, no matter how much experience you have online, you'll find plenty to amuse, inform, offend, and confuse on Usenet. This environment is so big and so rich in information that you can't possibly absorb it all. That's why it makes sense to start slowly, and become part of the newsgroups that really interest you. If the Internet gets to be too much, drop by alt.angst.

Telnet: Long-Distance Computing

Let's say you teach in Des Moines and want to search the Library of Congress catalogs in Washington, D.C. for information about public housing. How would you proceed? Or you're enrolled in college and need to research the impact of nutritional labeling on the marketing of food products. Let's just say you want to play a game of go, chess, or backgammon, or play in some MUD. You'd begin your Internet search with *telnet*, the Internet tool for logging on to and using any of hundreds of computers on the Internet.

The reason to use remote computers is that they often have things your own computer lacks. One computer might have a special Internet service, such as an archie server. Another might have a card catalog for a library, a database, or a community bulletin board. Another lets you compile programs or use a supercomputer, or keeps you abreast of job offerings or farm conditions.

If you've ever used other online service providers, you've probably experienced the inconvenience of logging on to remote systems and then typing Unix-style commands at prompts. Telnet is in fact a fairly primitive Internet tool. Because you are completely dependent on the remote computer, it is impossible to put a consistent or particularly friendly interface on all your telnet sessions; the remote computers differ, as do the programs you use remotely. Worst of all, when these computers are in heavy demand, performance can slow to a stop.

NetCruiser's telnet program frees you to some extent from the tyranny of the command line interface and provides you with a familiar window in which to interact with distant computers. It's a tool that takes much of the pain out of telnet. In this chapter you'll learn about telnet and the Net-Cruiser telnet program, and you'll visit some useful telnet sites.

Using NetCruiser's Telnet Window

With NetCruiser you make a connection to a remote system in one of two ways: by selecting a host site address from the addresses NetCruiser provides at the Internet Site Chooser, or (the better way) by directly typing in the specific site address in the Site Chooser's Site box.

To access a telnet site, follow these steps:

1. With NetCruiser running, select Internet ➤ Telnet-Remote Login or click on the Telnet icon on the NetCruiser toolbar:

The Site Chooser opens, displaying the map of the United States that's shown in Figure 4.1.

2. If you use the drop-down box to select a site in a certain state, scroll down the list until you find the address you want, then click on it. If you already know the address, just type it in the Site box. In either case, change the port number in the Port box if it's different from the default. After you enter an address or select an address from the list, press ↵ or click on OK to connect.

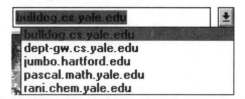

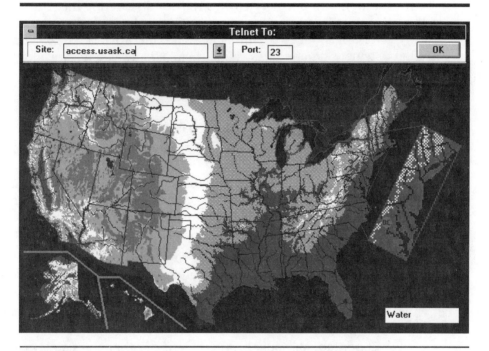

FIGURE 4.1: After you select the telnet tool, NetCruiser displays a map of the United States to help you locate telnet site addresses.

Finding Telnet Addresses

The NetCruiser Site Chooser—that big map—is fine when you want to connect to a specific telnet site. However, cyberspace extends beyond the boundaries of the United States. Furthermore, the Internet is dotted with many roadside attractions—smaller or newer online library catalogs, databases, bulletin boards, and other public information resources, which might not be included on the map.

Click on Canada to see a list of telnet sites **anywhere** outside the U.S.

The next section introduces hytelnet, a tool for discovering the telnet addresses of hundreds of libraries and assorted other information centers. Then you'll learn about LIBS, a program that both provides a direct connection to telnet sites and takes you to them. Finally, you'll learn about Yanoff's list, which you can browse from LIBS. Hytelnet and LIBS are themselves telnet sites.

Discovering Telnet Sites with Hytelnet

Hytelnet is a database of computerized library catalogs and other information services available through telnet. It provides a fairly complete listing of telnet site addresses that's updated frequently. The menu-driven program includes community free-nets, BBS's, and other information sources.

A free-net is an Internet institution—a community-based bulletin board service (BBS) or other computer system, usually with a School, a Town Hall, a Recreation Center, a Library, and more. The free-nets of Cleveland, Victoria (British Columbia), Cupertino, Milwaukee, and dozens of other cities are available to the world via Internet. See "Free-nets" later in this chapter, where you'll visit one.

To access hytelnet, type **access.usask.ca** in the Site box, and press ↵ or click OK. That's all you have to do to connect. The screen displays the information that appears in Figure 4.2.

```
Telnet To: access.usask.ca

ULTRIX V4.3 (Rev. 44) (access.usask.ca)

login: hytelnet
```

FIGURE 4.2: Once you connect to hytelnet, the program asks you to enter a login name. Logging on is a standard part of just about every telnet session.

 Telnet is character-based. To improve the way characters look on your screen, select Settings ➤ Telnet Options, and click the Font button. Choose the font type, size, and style you prefer, and click OK.

Telnet Addressing Conventions

When you want to connect to hytelnet, you specify its computer name, access.usask.ca, as you entered above. You could also use its IP address, 128.233.3.1. Both addresses work, and both use the same Internet addressing convention you use to send a mail message. The address composed of words is called a *domain name address,* and the address composed of numbers is called the *IP address.*

 It's easier to remember the domain name. Also, the domain name is less likely to change than the IP address. See "Anatomy of an Address" in Chapter 2.

Logging On to Hytelnet

Once you connect to the hytelnet program, the screen prompts you to enter your login name. Log in by typing **hytelnet** and pressing ↵. You'll see a menu system like the one that's shown in Figure 4.3.

You might want to play with the system in order to get used to its conventions, and perhaps get out a pen and paper to keep track of them. You'll

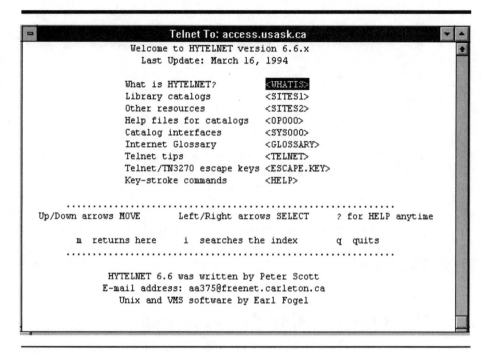

```
┌──────────────────────────────────────────────────────────────┐
│ ─               Telnet To: access.usask.ca            ▼ ▲     │
│                Welcome to HYTELNET version 6.6.x        ▲     │
│                  Last Update: March 16, 1994                  │
│                                                              │
│              What is HYTELNET?        <WHATIS>               │
│              Library catalogs         <SITES1>              │
│              Other resources          <SITES2>              │
│              Help files for catalogs  <OP000>              │
│              Catalog interfaces       <SYS000>             │
│              Internet Glossary        <GLOSSARY>          │
│              Telnet tips              <TELNET>            │
│              Telnet/TN3270 escape keys <ESCAPE.KEY>     │
│              Key-stroke commands      <HELP>            │
│                                                        │
│       ...............................................  │
│    Up/Down arrows MOVE      Left/Right arrows SELECT      ? for HELP anytime │
│                                                        │
│       m  returns here      i  searches the index      q  quits │
│       ...............................................  │
│                                                        │
│              HYTELNET 6.6 was written by Peter Scott  │
│              E-mail address: aa375@freenet.carleton.ca │
│              Unix and VMS software by Earl Fogel      │
│                                                        │
└──────────────────────────────────────────────────────────────┘
```

FIGURE 4.3: Hytelnet provides you with menu choices to help you get the information—a domain-name address—for a particular site.

probably discover some unexpected telnet services that you'll want to explore later—and you'll need to write down their telnet addresses.

Finding a Telnet Address Using Hytelnet

Once you connect to hytelnet, the first choice on the screen, *<WHATIS>*, is highlighted; select it to find out what hytelnet is (or just keep reading). Use ↓ and ↑ to move the cursor among the choices. Press → or ↵ to make a selection. You'll get another menu, which in turn will display information telling you how to connect to sites and giving any special commands or instructions you might need. To move back to where you started (for example, from a submenu to the main menu), press the ← on your computer.

For example, suppose you want to locate the telnet address for the Dartmouth College Library Online System. Follow these steps to find the information:

1. From the opening hytelnet menu, select *Library catalogs <SITES1>*.

2. From the *On-Line Library Catalogs* submenu, choose *The Americas* ➤ *United States* ➤ *Other Libraries*. A list of U.S. libraries now appears.

As you move from one hytelnet menu to another, it may seem as if you're not going anywhere or moving very slowly. Occasionally, when network activity is busy, you might experience a delay—sometimes a long delay—between the time you type a command or enter a request and the time the remote service responds. (You type commands instead of using the mouse because the application you're connected to by telnet is running on the remote computer.)

3. Press the spacebar to scroll through the list of libraries. Continue pressing the spacebar until you see Dartmouth University. Press → or ↵ to select the choice. The screen displays access information about Dartmouth's library, as shown in Figure 4.4. The library's address is lib.dartmouth.edu, its IP address is provided as well, and there is in this case the name and e-mail address of someone to contact for information about this site.

The later in the evening you connect, the faster your response time will be. As a test, I used both a 2400 and 14,400 baud rate modem (on two different computers) to see if there would be any significant difference in performance. I assumed there would be but I was wrong. When I initiated a connection at 2:00 p.m. PST, both modems responded slowly. I couldn't tell the difference. Only in the late evening, did the 14.4 modem respond significantly faster than the 2400 modem. Also remember to keep in mind the time-zone you're working in. The time of day when you connect, say, from the west coast to the east coast, can greatly affect performance.

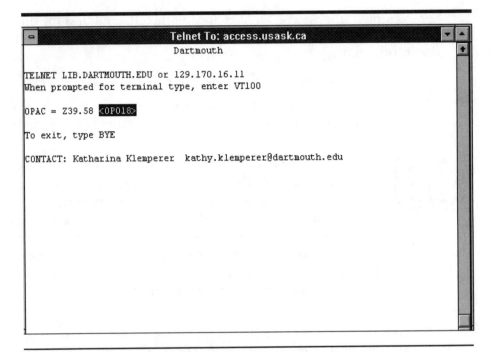

FIGURE 4.4: After you make your selection, the screen displays the address information you want. Dartmouth's address is lib.dartmouth.edu.

Exiting Hytelnet

You can continue to search for other telnet addresses or you can disconnect. To disconnect from hytelnet and return to your system, hit your q key to quit. The *escape character*, Ctrl+], is also good to remember.

When all else fails, pressing Ctrl+] will usually disconnect you from a telnet session and then return you to NetCruiser.

A Step Further: Connecting with LIBS

The LIBS program actually connects you to Internet services through telnet. It's similar to the hytelnet program, but more convenient to use. You can use the program in two ways. First (like hytelnet), you can use it to access a list of Internet resources. Second (unlike hytelnet), you can connect *directly* to many Internet resources and services with it.

The LIBS interface provides a well-designed menu from which to make your choices and clear instructions for using the program.

To access the program through NetCruiser, open the Site Chooser and type **nessie.cc.wwu.edu** in the Site box.

This address connects you to a computer at Western Washington University. Once you make the connection, log on by typing **LIBS** at the login prompt and pressing ⏎. Enter **VT100** as your terminal emulation type (or press ⏎ to display a list of other choices). The program's opening screen appears, displaying the main menu that's shown in Figure 4.5.

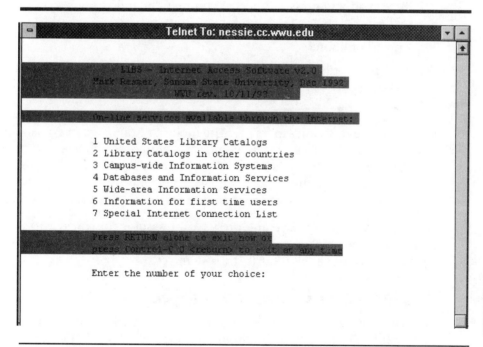

FIGURE 4.5: The LIBS program's main menu displays a list of online services that are available through the Internet. From here, you can find out the weather in Atlanta, do a search of a library in Honolulu, explore FDA AIDS briefings, and much more.

Here's how you would access Dartmouth's online library using the LIBS telnet connection:

1. Choose 1, United States Libraries, from the menu and then press ↵.

2. Select 27, New Hampshire, from the menu and press ↵. Dartmouth is the only New Hampshire library online.

3. Type y and press ↵ to have the LIBS program make a connection for you. When you get through you'll see a welcome message.

Once you're connected to the Dartmouth University Online System, you can conduct a search of its extensive catalog file. Let's say you want to find information on nutritional labeling, but you don't have a specific title in mind. At the bottom of the screen you'll see a command menu you use to search the catalog. To conduct a search by title, follow these steps:

1. Type **find** and press ↵. Another command menu appears.

2. Enter **title**. You can also search for a topic, author, or other information, as prompted.

3. Type the word(s) you want to search for, in this case **Nutritional Labeling**. The system notifies you that it's searching the catalog.

After a wait, the system displays the results of the search: one item with the phrase you're seeking in its file. The modest results suggest you should broaden the search to *labeling*, or change the kind of search from *title* to *subject*, since not all books' subjects are reflected in their titles. The search, *find subject labeling*, returns 142 items (see Figure 4.6). Some are irrelevant to nutritional labeling, but more than one does deal with that subject.

To exit the system, type **bye** and press ↵. At the submenu, press ↵ to see the previous menu. Keep pressing ↵ until you return to the LIBS program's main menu. However, don't exit the system yet.

Finding Telnet Sites by Subject

With LIBS you can make a direct connection to a specific library. But what if you want to search for information on a specific subject but don't know *where* to look? LIBS can help you locate specific telnet addresses by subject. This service provides a convenient subject-oriented guide, based on

```
Search S2: FIND SUBJECT LABELING
Result S2: 142 items in the CATALOG file.

   1. Fritschler, A. L... Smoking and politics : policy making... 1989
   2. Likhtenshtein, G... Biophysical labeling methods in mole... 1993
   3. Institute of Med... Food labeling : toward national unif... 1992
   4. Salzman, James.    Environmental labelling in OECD coun... 1991
   5. United States. C... Cigarette labeling and advertising, ... 1969
   6.                   Colloidal gold : principles, methods... 1989
   7. Worrall, Anne.    Offending women : female lawbreakers... 1990
   8. Institute of Med... Nutrition labeling : issues and dire... 1990
   9.                   UN/ECE standards for fresh fruit and... 1988
  10. Ehn, Michael.     Abweichende Lebensgeschichten : ange... 1989
  11. NATO Advanced Re... Photochemical probes in biochemistry... 1989
  12. Gonzalez Vaque, ... Pesticide labelling legislation /     1988
  13. Hadden, Susan G.  Read the label : reducing risk by pr... 1986
  14.                   Nutrition information in the superma... 1985
  15. Schur, Edwin M.   Labeling women deviant : gender, sti... 1984
---------------------------------------------------------------------
Press RETURN to continue display, or type one of the following commands:
   DISPLAY SHORT      DISPLAY LONG      SELECT FILE      FIND       HELP
   DISPLAY MEDIUM     DISPLAY CIRC      CONNECT          BROWSE     BYE
-> 
   Type HELP for suggestions for restricting your search.
```

FIGURE 4.6:   A search for **subjects** pertaining to **labeling** yields 142 items.

Scott Yanoff's subject list. If you know the topic or subject, you can probably locate a telnet site that'll provide the information you want.

Although far from complete, the extensive list does provide you with a
directory of telnet addresses, plus some archie, FTP, and gopher addresses.
To access Yanoff's list, follow these steps:

1. From the LIBS main menu choose 7 from the main menu. A list of Internet services appears on your screen.

2. Press N (for Next page) and ↵ to display more listings (see Figure 4.7).

3. To exit, press Q. You'll return to the main LIBS menu.

At any time you can press Ctrl+] to exit LIBS. This keyboard shortcut inter-
rupts the program and returns you to NetCruiser.

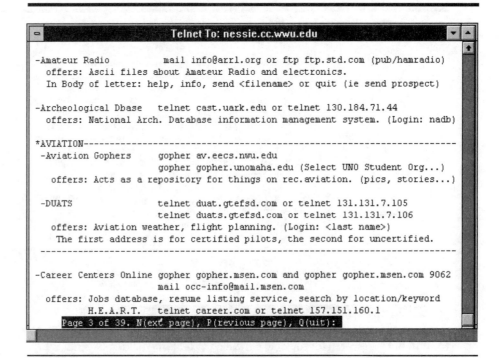

```
┌─────────────────────────────────────────────────────────────────┐
│ ─              Telnet To: nessie.cc.wwu.edu                  ▼  ▲ │
│                                                                ▲ │
│ -Amateur Radio          mail info@arrl.org or ftp ftp.std.com (pub/hamradio)│
│   offers: Ascii files about Amateur Radio and electronics.      │
│   In Body of letter: help, info, send <filename> or quit (ie send prospect)│
│                                                                 │
│ -Archeological Dbase   telnet cast.uark.edu or telnet 130.184.71.44│
│   offers: National Arch. Database information management system. (Login: nadb)│
│                                                                 │
│ *AVIATION--------------------------------------------------------│
│  -Aviation Gophers      gopher av.eecs.nwu.edu                  │
│                         gopher gopher.unomaha.edu (Select UNO Student Org...)│
│    offers: Acts as a repository for things on rec.aviation. (pics, stories...)│
│                                                                 │
│  -DUATS                 telnet duat.gtefsd.com or telnet 131.131.7.105│
│                         telnet duats.gtefsd.com or telnet 131.131.7.106│
│    offers: Aviation weather, flight planning. (Login: <last name>)│
│    The first address is for certified pilots, the second for uncertified.│
│   --------------------------------------------------------------│
│                                                                 │
│ -Career Centers Online gopher gopher.msen.com and gopher gopher.msen.com 9062│
│                    mail occ-info@mail.msen.com                   │
│    offers: Jobs database, resume listing service, search by location/keyword│
│         H.E.A.R.T.   telnet career.com or telnet 157.151.160.1  │
│   Page 3 of 39. N(ext page), P(revious page), Q(uit):           │
└─────────────────────────────────────────────────────────────────┘
```

FIGURE 4.7: Part of the Yanoff list of Internet services available on LIBS

Topics on Yanoff's list range from Agriculture to World-Wide Web. Take some time and browse the list. Table 4.1 provides quick access information for finding resources under major categories. Use the table to locate selected telnet sites.

If you want to keep track of new telnet sites as they come on-line, check out the Washington & Lee gopher (you'll learn about gopher searches in Chapter 6). Its gopher address is liberty.uc. wlu.edu.

Don't count on a computer to give you online directions for getting around and getting off. Do some research first, and if you have an e-mail address for a site, get in touch with someone responsible for a system (often available at the startup screen) before attempting to use it.

TABLE 4.1:   Telnet Services by Category

SERVICE	ADDRESS	LOGIN	DESCRIPTION
Agriculture			
Agriculture	idea.ag.uiuc.edu	flood	Agricultural information, livestock reports, current market prices, etc.
Careers			
Careers	career.com	your name, as prompted	Search for jobs by company, position, or state
Consumer Services			
Consumer Access Services	columbia.ilc.com *or* 38.145.77.221	cas	Product reports, evaluations, ratings; also bibliographic information
Economics/Business			
Economics	infopath.ucsd.edu	infopath	News & Services	Economic Bulletin Board
Business	a2i.rahul.net	guest	Stock market reports
Education/Teaching/Learning			
Teaching	nysernet.org	empire	K–12 resources, discussion groups, etc.

TABLE 4.1: Telnet Services by Category (continued)

SERVICE	ADDRESS	LOGIN	DESCRIPTION
Education	nis.calstate.edu	intl	International education BBS program, listings, resources, government information
Learning Link	sierra.fwl.edu	newuser	Electronic information on education and communication service
Law			
Law Library	liberty.uc.wlu.edu	lawlib	A listing of law libraries and legal research facilities
LawNet	lawnet.law.columbia.edu	lawnet	Law/judicial information and access to library catalogs
Medical/Health/Biology/Genetics			
Educational Tech Net	etnet.nlm.nih.gov	etnet	Forums and discussion groups on medical technology and education
Health	bongo.cc.utexas.edu	tatp	Finding disability assistance, equipment, services

TABLE 4.1: Telnet Services by Category (continued)

SERVICE	ADDRESS	LOGIN	DESCRIPTION
Politics/Government			
Air Pollution BBS	ttnbbs.rtpnc.epa.gov		Various BBSs that cover a wide range of air pollution information
Unix			
Public-Access Unix	nyx.cs.du.edu	new	Free account, with access to various Unix features
Judaica			
JewishNet	vms.huji.ac.il (in Israel)	jewishnet	Information on mailing lists, restaurants, Hebrew software, and more
Science/Math/Statistics			
E-Math	e-math.ams.com	e-math	The American Mathematics Society BBS, with software and reviews
GAMS	gams.nist.gov	gams	Guide to available mathematical software

TABLE 4.1: Telnet Services by Category (continued)

SERVICE	ADDRESS	LOGIN	DESCRIPTION
Stis	stis.nsf.gov	public	Science and technology information system
Software/Information Servers			
Software Server	rusinfo.rus.uni-stuttgart.de	info	Journals, Unix utilities, recipes, online cookbook, etc.
Software Server (ASK)	askhp.ask.uni-karlsruhe.de	ask	Online software search
Travel			
Subway Navigator	metro.jussieu.fr 10000		Information on subway routes of major cities, in French or English
Weather/Atmospheric/Oceanic			
Weather	oes1.oes.ca.gov 5501		State of California Governor's Office of Emergency Services
Flood	exnet.iastate.edu	flood	A lot of files on coping with floods and hurricanes
Weather Services	downwind.sprl.umich.edu		Information on world weather patterns

Making the Most of Online Library Systems

Hundreds of libraries from the Snohomish Public Library in Washington State to the Library of Congress make their collections (or at least their card catalogs) available on the Internet.

Why would you want to search a library collection that you can't access in person? The answer is simple: time, distance, and money. It's not easy to visit the Library of Congress if you live in New Mexico. Telnet provides you with tools to conduct some basic bibliographic research before you head down to your local branch library to check out what you need.

 Most library research you do using telnet is bibliographic. That is, you can compile a list of books and authors, but not see actual books online. There are hundreds of books online, but nothing like the millions that could be online. See "Good Books, and Free" in Chapter 6.

In these days of library closures, limited hours of operation, and dwindling collections, we're starting to see a consolidation of library resources. Cities can no longer support numerous neighborhood branches. Fewer libraries means less access to resources. The Internet provides us with alternative forms of access to the information once made available by your public library—without a library card.

Melvyl: Ten Million and Counting

Melvyl is the online card catalog of the massive University of California library system, which serves nine campuses and has over 11 million holdings. Its address is melvyl.ucop.edu.

Telnet Conventions

The following rituals are common in most telnet sessions, so it's a good idea to get used to them.

Logging In After you enter the telnet address and connect to the site of your choice, follow the onscreen instructions for using the particular system. Different systems have their own conventions, so you'll need to read the instructions carefully—if they're available online at all. You probably need to enter a login name, sometimes a password, and often terminal emulation information as well. Be sure you know your login before you start!

Terminal Emulation Mainframe and Unix systems usually ask you to enter the *terminal emulation* setting you're using. Terminal emulation enables your computer to connect to the host computer, by making your computer behave like a type of computer, or terminal, that the host computer can communicate with. Usually the host will provide you with a list of terminal emulation settings from which to choose. The NetCruiser telnet tool emulates a vt100 terminal, so choose **vt100** at the remote computer. If you have problems, select Settings ➤ Telnet Options and make sure the Terminal Emulation box is set to *VT100*.

Navigation Ways of getting around remote computers differ, but you usually use arrow keys, and they usually take you in the direction you'd expect. You can usually select menu items using ↵, and backtrack using ←.

Getting Out You can usually log off (or quit) a connection with a remote computer by selecting *Exit* or *Quit* from a menu or typing **bye** or **quit** at a prompt. You can also end the connection by closing the telnet window: double click the Control menu box in the upper-left corner of the telnet window. (The telnet window has a fixed size, so its Control menu is distinct from NetCruiser's.)

When you connect with Melvyl, you'll see the screen shown in Figure 4.8. Enter *VT100* as your terminal emulation type.

To get started, just press ↵. You don't need to enter a user id. A catalog menu appears on the screen, as shown in Figure 4.9. You are prompted to enter your choice from the menu.

If you want to look up something on Melvyl's system-wide catalog, enter **CAT** to access the catalog file. The screen prompts you to enter a command to conduct a search. The menu provides you with command options. Let's see whether the Melvyl catalog does any better on the subject of *labeling* than the Dartmouth catalog. To begin a search, select an option from the menu and type the command at the prompt. You can use either

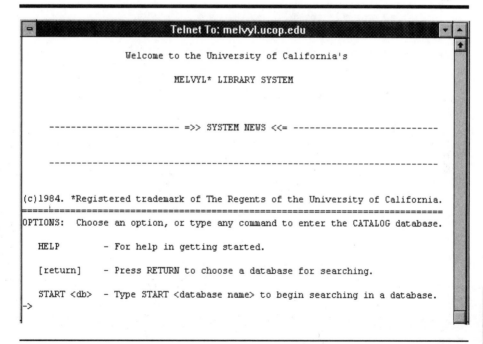

FIGURE 4.8: This opening screen appears when you connect to Melvyl, the University of California library system's electronic card catalog.

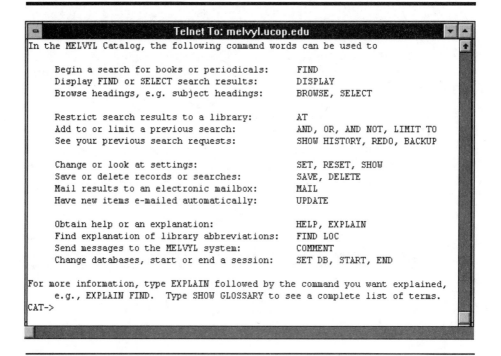

```
─  ▼  Telnet To: melvyl.ucop.edu                    ▼ ▲
In the MELVYL Catalog, the following command words can be used to    ↑

    Begin a search for books or periodicals:    FIND
    Display FIND or SELECT search results:      DISPLAY
    Browse headings, e.g. subject headings:     BROWSE, SELECT

    Restrict search results to a library:       AT
    Add to or limit a previous search:          AND, OR, AND NOT, LIMIT TO
    See your previous search requests:          SHOW HISTORY, REDO, BACKUP

    Change or look at settings:                 SET, RESET, SHOW
    Save or delete records or searches:         SAVE, DELETE
    Mail results to an electronic mailbox:      MAIL
    Have new items e-mailed automatically:      UPDATE

    Obtain help or an explanation:              HELP, EXPLAIN
    Find explanation of library abbreviations:  FIND LOC
    Send messages to the MELVYL system:         COMMENT
    Change databases, start or end a session:   SET DB, START, END

For more information, type EXPLAIN followed by the command you want explained,
    e.g., EXPLAIN FIND.  Type SHOW GLOSSARY to see a complete list of terms.
CAT->
```

FIGURE 4.9: Melvyl's main command menu.

upper- or lowercase. Type **find subject labeling** and press ↵. Figure 4.10 shows part of the result of the search, which yielded 449 entries.

Press D to display bibliographic information. To *see* an item you still have to go to a library of the UC system.

Most library systems tell you how to log off and return to your host system. To exit Melvyl type **quit**. To leave LIBS, follow the prompts.

Colorado Alliance of Research Libraries

The Colorado Alliance of Research Libraries (CARL) is a valuable online library system for a *group* of libraries. It maintains a public access catalog of services, encyclopedias, and databases for libraries throughout Colorado,

```
Search request: FIND SUBJECT LABELING
Search result:  449 records at all libraries

Type HELP for other display options.

18. Block, Zenas.
       It's all on the label : understanding food, additives, and nutrition /
    Zenas Block.  1st ed.  Boston : Little, Brown, c1981.
         UCB    BioSci    TX553.A3 .B58
         UCD    Shields   TX553.A3 B58
         UCI    Main Lib  TX553.A3 B58
         UCLA   URL       TX 553 A3 B58
         UCSD   Central   TX553.A3 B58
         UCSD   Undergrad TX553.A3 B58

19. The Brand name food game / [compiled by the editors of] Consumer guide.
    [New York : New American Library, 1974].
       Series title:  Signet reference.
         UCB    BioSci    S21 .A796 Shelved at BIOSCIENCES OFF CAMPUS COLLECTION




Press RETURN to see next screen. Type PS to see previous screen.
CAT-> █
```

FIGURE 4.10: The results of a search for holdings that have to do with the subject of labeling. Melvyl found 449 holdings—three times as many as the Dartmouth search (Figure 4.6).

the West, and as far east as Boston. To connect to CARL, enter **pac.carl.org** in the Site Chooser's address box.

Once you're connected, type **PAC** at the login prompt and then identify your terminal. (PAC stands for Public Access Catalog.) When the main menu appears on screen, choose 4, Other Library Systems. At the next submenu, choose 42, Western US, which includes public, academic, and school library catalogs, and some local information databases. When the screen displays the next submenu, Library Catalogs–Western United States, select the Pikes Peak Library System, which serves the city of Colorado Springs.

Several years ago, the librarians of Pikes Peak realized they could use their database program not just for books but for cataloging city records and community information as well. As you can see in Figure 4.11, the Pikes Peak Library System District provides useful information on municipal

```
┌─────────────────────────────────────────────────────────────────┐
│ ▫            Telnet To: pac.carl.org                       ▼ ▲    │
│                                                              ↑    │
│                                                                   │
│                                                                   │
│   Pikes Peak Library District offers the following information:   │
│                                                                   │
│       1.  PPLD On-Line Card Catalog                               │
│                                                                   │
│       2.  Community Connections: Menu of Community Information Databases │
│                                                                   │
│       3.  Encyclopedia, Business and Reference Sources            │
│                                                                   │
│                                                                   │
│       5.  Menu of Government Databases, including City Hall On-Line │
│             and Colorado Legislative Database                     │
│                                                                   │
│       6.  Menu of Other Library Systems                           │
│                                                                   │
│       7.  Help and Library News                                   │
│                                                                   │
│                                                                   │
└─────────────────────────────────────────────────────────────────┘
```

FIGURE 4.11: CARL provides public access to a number of online library catalog systems, such as the one for the Pikes Peak Library District.

ordinances and other city records. You type in the word you're searching for and the online catalog cites the relevant laws or decisions.

CARL will also connect you to the University of Hawaii library, which, like the one in Colorado Springs, has more than just bibliographic material online. One of its features is an online Hawaiian almanac that can tell you everything you ever wanted to know about Hawaiians, including the average number injured in boogie-board accidents each year (seven).

Free-nets

Telnet also gives you access to *free-nets*, community-based networks that have sprung up across North America—in Washington D.C., Wyoming (the Big Sky Telegraph), Cleveland, Victoria, B.C., Cleveland, and elsewhere. They offer local members resources such as conferencing, e-mail, information services, and interactive communications, in the framework of a virtual community; non-residents are sometimes restricted in what they can do. This type of BBS is usually free, which is the reason for its name, but you can incur a nominal fee if you don't live in the community but want to use certain services.

 Most free-nets are in the first place community organizations, and as a visitor your access to certain services, such as mail, might be limited.

The Cleveland Free-net was the first of its kind. It represented an ambitious attempt to bring the Internet to the public. Originally an in-hospital help network, it's now sponsored by Case Western Reserve University, the city of Cleveland, the state of Ohio, and IBM. It uses simple menu systems, similar to those found on other online services such as CompuServe and GEnie, to provide a broad range of community and informational services.

The Cleveland Free-net has a vast and growing collection of public documents, from copies of U.S. and Ohio Supreme Court decisions to the Magna Carta and the U.S. Constitution. It links residents to various government agencies and has daily stories from *USA Today*. It also maintains a large collection of local conferences. For students it offers a rich set of books, activities, and discussion areas.

To connect to the Cleveland Free-net through telnet, you can use any one of the following addresses:

- ◆ freenet-in-a.cwru.edu
- ◆ freenet-in-b.cwru.edu
- ◆ freenet-in-c.cwru.edu

When you connect, log on as a visitor and look around the system. If you want to be able to post messages in its conferences or use e-mail, you will have to apply in writing for an account. Information on accounts is available when you connect.

A number of other cities also maintain their own free-nets, including Youngstown, Ohio. Its free-net is called the Youngstown Free-net. To connect through telnet, type **yfn.ysu.edu** in the Site box. At the login prompt, type **visitor** and press ↵. You can browse through the system to see what it has to offer.

The Flavors of MUD

Telnet gives you a gateway to almost all Internet services. For example, you can log on to an archie server using telnet and search FTP sites for a specific file. You can also start a World Wide Web session at info.cern.ch (log in as **www**), or read Usenet news at kufacts.cc.ukans.edu (log in as **kufacts**). But because telnet consumes the resources of remote computers, it's faster and more efficient to use the NetCruiser News reader or Web browser.

Telnet also gives you access to the world of online interactive games, such as Go, bridge, chess, and MUD (multi-user dimension). In a MUD you construct imaginary realities with other people online. There are all sorts of MUDs, with names like Apocalypse, Nemesis, and tinyMUD.

Game sites come and go and can be busy to the point of uselessness, so it's best to do some homework first. You can find out about the latest, best, and most accessible telnet sites by visiting one of the relevant Usenet newsgroups, such as rec.games.chess or rec.games.mud, which has a dozen or so subgroups (rec.games.mud.*). There, you can also share your experiences and get answers to your burning questions.

Telnet makes rich resources available to students, teachers, farmers, travelers, hackers, job seekers, and probably for you as well. Happy telnetting!

FTP: Files to Go

FTP—short for *file transfer protocol*—is the Internet tool that lets you browse remote computers and download files that you need, or are just curious about, to use on your own computer. The beauty of FTP is that the files are free for the taking. And if you have appropriate permissions on a remote computer, such as Netcom's, you can upload files for others to use. That kind of sharing is how FTP got started in the first place.

There are probably as many reasons to use FTP as there are people using the Internet. Maybe you want to…

> …download some anti-virus software (which you *should* do if you plan to download a lot of files).
>
> …make the document you just wrote on your word-processor available to a colleague.
>
> …get some game software for your PC.
>
> …continue your research on earthquakes in the western United States by downloading some data files gathered from remote sensors and stored on a file server.
>
> …collect NASA photos of quasars.

These are the sorts of activities for which people use FTP. You'll probably find your own.

If you have any experience using Unix FTP—typing in commands and watching lists of files zip by; losing your way in the unfamiliar directory structures of different computers—NetCruiser will make the whole process simpler than you could have imagined. NetCruiser gives you a better over-view of the remote computer's structure, and when you download files, they come straight to your PC. You no longer have to fool around with the Kermit and Zmodem protocols to get files from your Internet host to your own PC. This chapter provides all you need to know to use Net-Cruiser's FTP tool to search for and retrieve files. At the end of the chapter you'll find a sampler of great FTP sites you can explore on your own.

What Is FTP?

With FTP you can transfer files *from* your computer to some other com-puter—*upload* them. You can also transfer files *to* your computer from some other computer—*download* them. If you're like most people you're more likely to download than upload.

You can transfer all kinds of files. *Text*, or ASCII, files are the files you can read, such as books and Usenet articles; they consist of letters and ordi-nary characters. *Binary* files include pictures, sound files, and executable programs.

When you transfer a file you must tell the FTP server who you are. The login id and password sequence are similar to the sequence you use when logging on to one of Netcom's computers. In fact, you may want to con-nect to Netcom's servers to download files. Netcom also makes directory space available if you want to upload files for the world to see. In *anony-mous FTP* you have access to remote sites even when you are not specifi-cally identified to the FTP server.

What Is Anonymous FTP?

Most of the FTP work (and play) you do with NetCruiser will involve downloading files, and downloading them by a method called anony-mous FTP.

Why Are There So Many Files Out There for the Taking?

FTP was developed so that the scientists using the military's ARPANET could share data with each other. In the 1970s and 1980s the National Science Foundation (NSF) designed a network called NSFNET that was like ARPANET but intended for nonmilitary projects such as calculating weather patterns and designing space satellites.

Since not all researchers were located at places with extensive research computing facilities, the NSF thought that researchers could share supercomputing facilities. So, the NSF funded six supercomputing facilities and made them available via a high-speed network linked to universities. The researchers used telnet to log in to the supercomputers; e-mail to work with others at the remote site and elsewhere; and FTP to send data and to bring the results back to their home institution. These were the first big uses of NSFNET, now the most important part of the Internet backbone.

The idea of sending files over the network instead of mailing computer tapes quickly caught on in universities. Long-distance research teams could find and copy the same information from one source at their convenience. Everyone could have the same data. The transfer was faster (even at the much slower speeds of the network at that time), and researchers got the data when they needed it.

Today, even with the increased use of gopher and World Wide Web, 40% of the traffic ("packets") on NSFNET is still FTP traffic. Applications such as gopher and Web use FTP because many data files (like information from the space program or weather information) are very, very large, and FTP remains an efficient way of moving files.

Anonymous FTP allows you to copy data to your own computer without requiring that you have a login id or account on every machine that might have files you want. This is a benefit to you and to the host site. You don't need to remember a lot of accounts and passwords, and the host site doesn't need to manage additional accounts. It also provides better security for a host site's private files.

It's called *anonymous* because the login id that you enter is, literally, **anonymous**. Using anonymous FTP with NetCruiser simplifies the process further: When you connect with an anonymous FTP site, the login and password (your mail address) are automatically sent to the site for *authorization*—permission to use the site.

What Kind of Files Can You Transfer?

Any kind of file you can store on a computer can be moved to another computer using FTP:

Text files	Any ASCII file—mailing lists, notes, README files, articles from Usenet news, etc.
Graphic images	.TIF (tagged image file), .GIF (graphics interchange format), .BMP (bit-mapped), or .JPEG formats. To view these files you need a viewer like the JPEG/GIF/BMP viewer in NetCruiser. You can also use a conversion program to use them in a graphics package.
Data in proprietary formats	FTP doesn't *read* raw data; it just packages it and moves it to the other machine. This is an advantage for you, since you don't have to describe the format in order to move the data.
Audio, video, and sound formats	FTP doesn't know (or care) what the files contain.
Program files	Executable code. Executable code may need to be relinked and may well need program libraries, many of which you can transfer with FTP, too.

Using NetCruiser to Download Files

NetCruiser brings unparalleled simplicity to anonymous FTP. Downloading files is now about as easy as using Windows' File Open dialog box, the point-and-click way of opening files in most Windows applications.

 If you want to upload files, you'll need the appropriate permissions on the remote computer. NetCruiser's Help system tells you how to upload.

Before you download a file you will need to know the following:

◆ The *address* of the FTP site. At the end of this chapter are instructions for using archie to discover the addresses of computers with the specific files you are searching for.

◆ The *name* of the file you are interested in (including the directory path).

◆ The *mode* you want to use (text or binary). This is easy if you know the extension. See Table 5.1.

TABLE 5.1:   File Extensions and File Types

FILE EXTENSION	FILE TYPE	RETRIEVAL MODE
.c	C programming language source code	Text/ASCII
.com	Executable files for DOS computers	Binary
.exe	Executable files for DOS or VAX/VMS computers	Binary
.gif	Graphics Interchange Format (compressed)	Binary

TABLE 5.1: File Extensions and File Types (continued)

FILE EXTENSION	FILE TYPE	RETRIEVAL MODE
.gz	Unix files that are compressed by the Unix GNU gzip utility program and will need to be processed before you will be able to use the files	Binary
.h	C programming language header files	Text/ASCII mode
.hqx	Compressed files for the Macintosh computer	Binary, then processed by a Macintosh uncompression program
.jpg	Graphics files in a compressed format	Binary
.mpeg, .mpg	Video files—they need to be viewed with a special software	Binary
.ps	PostScript files, must be viewed with a PostScript viewer or printed on a PostScript printer	Text/ASCII
.sit	Macintosh files processed by the Stuffit program	Binary
.tar	Unix files that are in the Unix tape archive format	Binary, then process with the Unix tar utility
.tar.Z	Unix files that are compressed tar files that require use of the uncompress utility, then the tar utility	Binary

TABLE 5.1: File Extensions and File Types (continued)

FILE EXTENSION	FILE TYPE	RETRIEVAL MODE
.txt	Files that have no special suffix are plain text files that can be displayed or printed without requiring processing by any utility	Text/ASCII
.Z	Unix files that are compressed	Binary, then run the Unix uncompress utility
.zip	DOS files compressed by a zip utility	Binary, then unzipped using a program such as Pkunzip

You start an FTP session by selecting Internet ➤ FTP Download or clicking on the FTP button in the NetCruiser toolbar.

As in telnet and gopher, a Site Chooser comes up, showing you a map of the United States. You can choose an FTP site by either typing it into the Site box or selecting it from a list of sites for a state that you have clicked (see Figure 5.1).

In the FTP To dialog box (see Figure 5.2), all the information required for logging on to an anonymous FTP site is filled in. Just click OK or press ↵ to accept the information and go to the site.

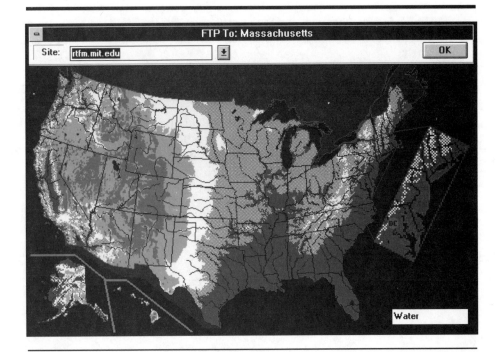

FIGURE 5.1: The Internet Site Chooser lets you choose an FTP site by either typing it in the Site box or selecting it from a drop-down list.

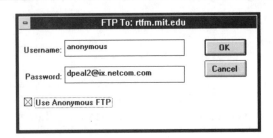

FIGURE 5.2: Dialog box with check box marked for anonymous FTP

By default, the check box marked Use Anonymous FTP in the lower left of the dialog box has an **X** in it, so NetCruiser logs you in as **anonymous** and places your e-mail address in the Password field. If you don't want to use the anonymous login, just click on the check box. NetCruiser then prompts you to use your regular Netcom login, or another one. Next, enter a password in the Password box. When you are satisfied that you have entered the correct information, press Enter or click OK.

If a site you have chosen is not in fact set up for anonymous FTP, you will get a dialog box telling you so, and you will be returned to the NetCruiser main window. If a site is busy (many allow only a certain number of people on at a time), you will, again, return to the main window.

If you get through, the FTP To window now comes up (see Figure 5.3).

Using the FTP To Window

The FTP To window gives you simple methods for getting an overview and moving around a remote computer. It makes it simple to view lists of files and directories, and to select a file or files to download.

The NetCruiser FTP To window has two major parts (or panes). The upper pane displays directories (folders for holding files); the lower pane, the files themselves.

At the bottom of the window you'll see the message display area—FTP's status bar. If the FTP server on the remote host sends back messages with many lines, those messages are displayed in a special pop-up window that you'll see on top of the FTP display. As with any window, you can move the message window to the back by clicking on the FTP display, or you can close it by pressing Ctrl+F4 or double-clicking the little box in the upper-left corner.

In the directory and file panes, if there are more directories or files than can fit in the pane, a scroll bar appears on the right side of the window. Like the Read My Mail window, you can resize the directory and file panes to show you more or fewer files at a time.

FTP: Files to Go

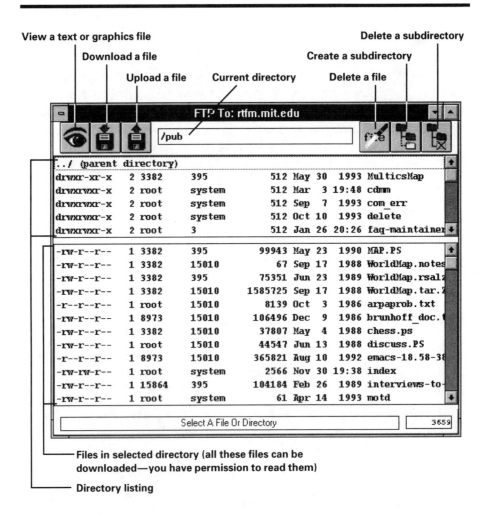

View a text or graphics file

Download a file

Upload a file

Current directory

Delete a subdirectory

Create a subdirectory

Delete a file

Files in selected directory (all these files can be downloaded—you have permission to read them)

Directory listing

FIGURE 5.3: The FTP To window is your control center in using anonymous FTP. The top part of the window displays directories; the bottom half, files for the selected directory. Double-clicking a file downloads it directly to your PC.

Each pane is ordered in rows. Information about both directories and files is structured in the same way. Four pieces of information are especially important to you (Figure 5.3). In order of importance (not the actual order!) they are:

Directory/ File name	The *last* element in the row of information about the directory or file. Items are ordered alphabetically by their names, with A–Z coming before a–z: *Apple* comes before *Zenith,* and both come before *arachnid* and *zooplankton.* You can learn something about a file from its type. (See "Figuring Out a File's Type from Its Name.") README files are text files that describe the kind of files you'll encounter in a particular directory.
File size, in bytes	Make sure you check file size before downloading a file, to get a sense of how long it will take and how much disk space it will require.
Permissions	That is, ability to use a file or directory; identified by a series of 10 characters at the start of every row. The first character shows a *d* if the item is a directory. A file has a dash (-) in this position. The next nine characters, in three groups of three characters, describe security permissions. *r* indicates permission to read a file or directory; *w* indicates permission to write to it (change it); *x* indicates permission to execute (run a program). Most of the time, all you have to worry about is the third group of three characters, which describes the permission set for the world, which includes everyone who has access to this host computer by anonymous FTP. For anonymous FTP to work, the *r* must be present in the eighth character position (see Figure 5.3). If you want to create, use, or delete a directory or file you must be able to write to it, and there must be a *w* in the ninth character position.

Date	The date that the file was last stored. If the file was modified in this calendar year, the time that the file was stored may be listed. Otherwise, the year that the file was modified is displayed.

 Permissions are set by the owner of a file (the person who made it available or who maintains it), not by the FTP program. The login process tells the remote FTP server who you are, so that it can determine your file privileges. If you try to access a file and FTP sends you a message denying access, you will need to get in touch with the owner of the file or someone at the site.

 Many anonymous FTP sites automatically display access information and a person to contact. Contact this person if you have questions about permission. Also, make sure to find the README file in the directory of concern to you.

Getting around the FTP Window

The box at the top of the FTP To window always shows you the directory you are in, and if you're in the root (top) directory, you will see a forward slash (/).

 Unlike DOS, Unix directories are marked with forward slashes (/), not backslashes (\).

You double-click a directory name in the Directory pane to show files for that directory. To move up a directory, you click

    ../ (parent directory)

in the Directory pane. This is the first line of that pane, so you may have to scroll to the top of the Directory pane to see it.

Figuring Out a File's Type from Its Name

The name of a file can tell you much about the file's type (whether it's text or binary).

The Internet connects computers of many types. In particular, data is available in formats readable by different types of computers. Files described as *text* are most likely going to be in the ASCII character set, which most computers can display for you. A file intended for a Unix machine *could* be transferred to a Macintosh, but *wouldn't* be usable. Think about what you're doing!

Table 5.1 should help you figure out what sort of file you are dealing with, and whether it makes sense to download it.

Compressed Files

Compression makes files much smaller, speeding up their transmission. Compression can reduce a graphics or text file to half of its original size, and other types of files can be reduced to as little as $1/20$th of their original size. A compressed file containing program source code will be about two-thirds its expanded size.

For more information, you can get the file **doc/pcnet/compression** at **ftp.cso.uiuc.edu** via anonymous FTP. It contains a comprehensive table listing the available file compression software and naming conventions. It is updated when new tools become available. You will find a complete list of all the compression schemes that are commonly used on PCs, Macintosh and Amiga computers, Unix workstations, and IBM mainframes. The file also lists the sites where you can find copies of the freeware and shareware programs that accomplish compression and decompression.

Compression is also known as *shrinking*, *stuffing*, *compacting*, and *zipping*. You'll see these terms in the names of the programs that actually do the compression and decompression. Table 5.1 helps you identify compressed files from their extensions. Note in Table 5.1 that some files—.GIFs for example—are already compressed.

You need a companion program to reverse the compression—you need to make sure that the decompression program accurately expands the stored codes. The compression document referred to in the previous tip has a list of FTP sites with this software. In fact, most large sites make it easy for you to find and download archive and compression programs. See, for example, the /pub/msdos/zip and /pub/msdos/arcers directories at oak.oakland.edu.

Files can be compressed only once. If you try to compress an already compressed file, it may end up bigger.

Downloading a Single File

If you just want to read a short file, such as a README file, and don't want to clutter up your hard disk, select a readable file, then click the View button. View will also display a .GIF, .JPEG, or text file.

If you decide to download a file, follow the steps below.

1. Double-click the file you want to download. The Select Transfer Mode dialog box comes up, where you tell NetCruiser the file's type: ASCII or Binary (see Figure 5.4). Choose ASCII for files that are text only {A-Z, a-z, the numbers 0-9 and assorted punctuation characters}. Choose Binary for pictures, graphic files, program code, and anything other than text. If a file is transferred in the wrong mode, the information is most likely to be damaged and you will need to redo the transfer. When in doubt, use binary.

2. Click either the Binary or ASCII button. Now you'll see the Windows Save As box, in which you tell NetCruiser what to call the file and in what directory to place it (see Figure 5.5).

3. Complete the box. NetCruiser suggests a name that conforms to the Windows file-naming conventions. Longer Unix file names will be converted to the eight-character file name, period, three-character extension-style name. Renaming a file is a good idea. Click OK.

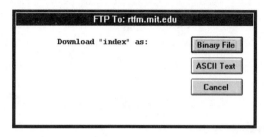

FIGURE 5.4:   This box asks you to tell the FTP site what kind of file you want to download, and how to send it. Table 5.1 can help you decide which one to use.

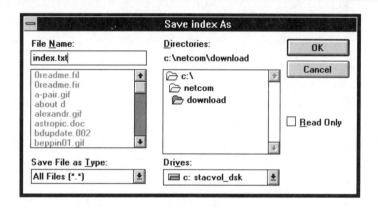

FIGURE 5.5:   Use the Save As box to name your file and give it a directory. If you don't name it, you run the risk of weird truncations.

The transfer to your machine begins. You can monitor its progress in the status bar, which displays the number of bytes already transferred as well as the number to be transferred. A message informs you whether the transfer is successfully completed.

226 Transfer complete.		14604

To use the file you've downloaded, you'll have to decompress it, if necessary, then open it within the appropriate word processor or graphics program.

To view a file you've downloaded, select File ➤ View Text File... or View Graphics File... and select the .GIF, .JPG, or text file you want to view.

Downloading Several Files at the Same Time

With NetCruiser you can select a group of files to download. But before you can select files, they must be visible in the directory window.

If you download more than one file with exactly the same name, such as README, the second file will overwrite the first, the third will overwrite the second, and so on. Download them one at a time and save them with different names.

To select two or more items *in sequence*, click on the first file or directory you want to select. Then press and hold down Shift while you click on the last file in the sequence.

To select two or more items *out of sequence*, press and hold down Ctrl while you click on each file.

If you've selected files you don't want, cancel your selection by taking your finger off Shift or Ctrl and clicking somewhere else.

You can also select multiple files with your *keyboard* using the arrow keys. First, move to the first file you want to select. Press and hold down Shift while selecting a sequence of files to download. To select two or more items *out of sequence* with the keyboard, use the arrow keys to move to the first file you want to select. Press and release Shift+F8. The mouse pointer bar will begin to blink. Use the arrow keys to move to the next item you want to select. Press the space bar to select each file or directory. Press Shift+F8 when you finish selecting files.

If you've selected files you don't want, you can cancel your selection. Press and release Shift+F8 so that the mouse pointer bar will begin to blink. Use the arrow keys to move to the selection you want to cancel, and then press the space bar. Press Shift+F8 when you finish canceling selections.

 Both the Select Transfer Mode and File Selection dialog boxes (asking you to choose Binary or ASCII) comes up for **each** file you select.

Pushing FTP's Buttons

NetCruiser's FTP window gives you pushbutton control over the program's major capabilities. If you have permission to upload files to a computer, you will especially appreciate the control NetCruiser gives you (see Figure 5.3).

 /pub/sybex

View   Fetches an ASCII, .GIF, or .JPEG file from the connected remote host and displays it. View works by downloading and displaying, but not saving, a file.

Download   Fetches a file from the connected remote host and stores it on your local computer.

Four other buttons—Upload, Delete, Make Directory, and Remove Directory—do pretty much what they say. If you had permission on a remote computer, you'd use these buttons to make and name directories, upload files for others to use, and delete files and directories you don't want to make available any more.

Practicing Safe Transfers

No matter how well managed an archive site is, accidents can happen. You should take precautions before installing and running any software you have transferred from another site.

Always run antivirus software on any new files, and scan your computer regularly for viruses. Be especially careful with game programs—tempting places for inconsiderate people to put viruses. Text and image files do not, as a rule, carry viruses.

If you are installing a program on your computer and your computer is itself on a local network, you will need to exercise special care because the mistake you make may well affect others. If you are in doubt of the consequences of your actions, check with you local system administrator. It is really important to do this if the program you are installing uses network resources. Your actions may not damage the work of others on your network, but you may consume more network resources than your administrator had anticipated, and you could possibly slow down everyone's access to data on your network.

Practicing Nice Transfers

FTP can be a large consumer of Internet resources. If you are going to transfer very large files, it is considerate to think about the effect of your action on others.

Try to locate the closest copy of the file. Usually, archie (the FTP utility for locating FTP sites—see the "Archie Primer" at the end of this chapter) returns more than one site with the same file. The farther a file travels, of course, the more resources it uses. A close file is one on your network. The next closest file is one on a Netcom network. The next closest is one on a host connected to a Netcom-connected network. You can't be expected to know who is connected this way, so don't spend a lot of time worrying about it—just be aware that a site across the street may be far away in networking terms.

If you are going to transfer lots of large files, space them out a bit, or transfer them at off-peak hours. Be aware that lots of people use the network during non-business hours. Some service providers (such as Netcom) charge less money to access the net in the evening or night, since folks who don't have access at work often connect at night. Think about when off-peak might be for the resource you are connecting to.

Great Anonymous FTP Sites

Here's a sampling of sites, presented in roughly alphabetical order, with files that might interest you. You can use anonymous FTP to log on to the sites and look around. After each site is a brief description of some of the things you might find there. Bear in mind that a file's name doesn't always reflect its contents. Of course, this list is far from comprehensive.

If you're just browsing, start your explorations in directories such as /pub, /gif, and /msdos.

Perry Rovers maintains a list of anonymous FTP sites. He posts it regularly to the following Usenet newsgroups:

alt.sources.wanted, alt.answers

comp.misc, comp.archives, comp.sources.wanted

news.answers, news.answers.questions

A good listing of sites with GIFs and other binary files is available at bongo.cc.utexas.edu and its path is /gifstuff/ftpsites.

While there are many, many host computers on the Internet, not all of them choose to support FTP. Those that do frequently allow anonymous FTP as a public service. Please remember that these connections, like other Internet resources, are finite. Don't stay connected to them any longer than you need to find the information you want.

Caveat Some of the host systems set restrictions on their FTP access. More than 10 connections (for example) will not be allowed. Or, service will only be given during business hours. Or, because the service is on a machine that is heavily loaded during business hours, connections will be refused until after hours. When this happens, FTP will display a message saying that the host is unavailable because there are too many connections, or that you should try again at some other (perhaps specified) time. You might be sent to an alternative site with the same holdings (some sites mirror each other's holdings). Remember that no Internet host is *required* to accept any connections at all. So be gracious about other people trying to manage their resources well.

Site	Description
ames.arc.nasa.gov	Space Archive, via NASA's Ames Research Center. Some good Voyager GIFs in /pub/gif.
andy.bgsu.edu	College hockey statistics. Bowling Green State (and the upper-Midwestern United States in general) have long been hotbeds of college hockey competition.
archie.au	Australian mirrored software archive (to reduce the traffic between the U.S. and Australia).

Mirroring really helps network and server congestion. If the mirror site is closer to you, you possibly will have a shorter response time. On the other hand, if your local server is busy because of the time of day, you might want to access one like this or one in Europe. Because of the time differences, the servers in other parts of the world may be less busy.

archive.nevada.edu	Included here are materials about the Constitution as well as about several religious organizations.

boombox. micro.umn.edu	The place to get gopher software. Go here, too, if you want to read more about gopher itself. You can get here and use FTP with gopher itself (see Chapter 6).
crvax.sri.com	RISKS Digest Archive. This archive contains information and discussions about computer security issues.
elbereth. rutgers.edu	Science fiction archive in /pub/sf1. This archive holds back discussions of the SF-lovers mailing list.
ftp.cwru.edu	In the /hermes directory you will find information about decisions handed down by the United States Supreme Court.
ftp.gsfc.nasa.gov	Hubble photos in /pub/images (Figure 5.6).

Gravitational Lens G2237+0305

FIGURE 5.6: Einstein's Cross. The quasar (center) is about 8 billion light years away. Its light is bent by the gravitational field of a galaxy only 400 million light years away, creating the appearance of 5 quasars, an effect called a **gravitational lens**. Courtesy of ftp.gsfc.nasa.gov.

ftp.eng.ufl.edu	Pictures of skydivers in /skydive/gifs (Figure 5.7).
ftp.ugcs. caltech.edu	Gorgeous photos of Pakistan in /pub/gifs (Figure 5.8).
ra.msstate.edu	Vietnam War photos in /pub/docs/history/usa/vietnam/gifs.

FIGURE 5.7: How did they do this? The file name is **54way**. Check out photos of other skydiving feats (over the Andes and elsewhere) at ftp.eng.ufl.edu.

FIGURE 5.8: The interior of the Mahabat Khan Mosque in Peshawar, Pakistan, one of a set of photographs shared by Pakistani students at Caltech at ftp.ugcs.caltech.edu.

ftp.ira.uka.de	Mandelbrot images in /pub/graphics.
ftp.eff.org	Info about Electronic Frontier Foundation. EFF is a membership organization that works to protect individual rights and promote good ethics on the Internet. Individual and corporate memberships are available. The *Big Dummy's Guide* is here in /pub/Net_info/Big_Dummy/. Stop off along the way (in /Net_info) for a wealth of information about the Internet.
ftp.exploratorium.edu	The Exploratorium, a hands-on science museum (see Chapter 7), has some of the Net's best images; note that they are copyrighted. Figure 5.9 shows an image (JPEG) from the museum.

ftp.lysator.liu.se	Science fiction archive.
ftp.nevada.edu	Virus information.
nic.funet.fi	Usenet University. Check this one out. Very large, miscellaneous holdings, including mirrors of Simtel and wuarchive. Good material about how to use the Internet.
ftp.ulowell.edu	The comp.binaries.ibm.pc Usenet newsgroup archives. Here's where you can download and upload PC software.
ftp.uu.net	Large software and Usenet news archive. Another site well worth browsing. Lots more for Unix people than for users of other types of computers, but the Net information is valuable.
pyrite.rutgers.edu	Security list archives. Another set of archives on computer security.
rtfm.mit.edu	Usenet news archive. Search here for the Usenet FAQs. For a list of Usenet newsgroups, check out /pub/usenet/ news.answers/active-newsgroups/part* (the asterisk stands for the multiple parts); for a list of mailing lists, check out /pub/usenet-by-group/news.answers/mail/ mailing-lists/part*.

The Public Domain Software Sites

Several sites are famous for their extensive collections of PC public domain (freeware and shareware) software. These sites are mirrored around the world. They contain software for IBM and compatible PCs running DOS or Windows; Macintosh and Apple IIs; Amigas; and Ataris.

FIGURE 5.9: Light, motion, and wonder—courtesy of the Exploratorium, in San Francisco. The Net is nothing like the real thing.

All of these sites are public services, generously supported by the owners of the institutions to which they are attached. Because these volunteer operations are run by charitable folks who are squeezing the resources from their primary missions, they must not be considered permanent. The collections themselves may disappear or move. The support for them may be lessened. The files may or may not be the latest versions, and in fact, may not be there at all. And different versions of the files may be on different servers. The contents of archive sites are not necessarily coordinated. But there is treasure here if you care to search.

ftp.cica.indiana.edu   Indiana Windows archive. This archive is widely considered to be the most comprehensive holding of public domain software for the Windows operating environment.

| oak.oakland.edu, wuarchive.wustl.edu | Oakland University in Rochester, Michigan and Washington University in St. Louis, Missouri—both have extensive miscellaneous collections. Online14.zip in /pub/msdos/info in Michigan is a shareware book by Odd de Presno, a Norwegian Internet guru. *The Online World* provides a European perspective on Internet issues. |

A Really Special Site: Ftp.netcom.com Users of Netcom's host dial service can request a special type of directory: their own anonymous FTP directory. This service provides a place to store files and make them available to the general public. If you look through the directory (by connecting using FTP to ftp.netcom.com, by browsing it with Netcom's gopher, or by browsing it with Netcom's World Wide Web page), you'll see many, many directories. Some are owned by companies who are making information about their products available in their FTP space. Some are owned by individuals who are sharing source code for programs, making their own private Web pages available, or leaving long joke files for their friends to discover. Browse the files. It's hard to predict what you'll find.

An Archie Primer

The sheer number of places to look and files available can make it hard to find the one file you need using anonymous FTP. Archie makes finding things easier.

Archie was developed at McGill University in Canada by a team of dedicated information junkies. They were trying to solve the same problem you are facing—where is the stuff I want? So, they built a program that searches the anonymous FTP sites of the Internet and builds a database of names of available files. This database is stored on the servers listed in Table 5.2. Using archie means asking an archie server where a certain file is; usually, archie will have pages of answers.

TABLE 5.2: Sites of Archie Servers

COMPUTER	LOCATION
archie.ans.net	ANS server, New York
archie.internic.net	AT&T server, New York
archie.rutgers.edu	Rutgers University, New Jersey
archie.sura.net	SURAnet server, Maryland
archie.unl.edu	U. of Nebraska
archie.au	Australia
archie.univie.ac.at	Austria
archie.edvz.uni-linz.ac.at	Austria
archie.uqam.ca	Canada
archie.funet.fi	Finland
archie.th-darmstadt.de	Germany
archie.ac.il	Israel
archie.unipi.it	Italy
archie.kuis.kyoto-u.ac.jp	Japan
archie.wide.ad.jp	Japan
archie.kr	Korea
archie.sogang.ac.kr	Korea
archie.nz	New Zealand
archie.rediris.es	Spain
archie.luth.se	Sweden
archie.switch.ch	Switzerland
archie.ncu.edu.tw	Taiwan
archie.doc.ic.ac.uk	United Kingdom

You communicate with an archie server in several ways:

◆ mail

◆ telnet

◆ archie client

 A NetCruiser archie client is in development. When it's ready, you'll be able to upgrade your software automatically when you log on, as described in Appendix B. For now, use mail or telnet to get access to archie.

Doing an Archie Search by Mail

You can send mail to any of the archie servers listed in Table 5.2. To send an archie query to the archie.ans.net server, for example, you address the mail to *archie@archie.ans.net*. The server reads the mail and replies by sending you mail with the results—names and addresses of computers from which you download a specific file. Each line of the mail message you send is a command; put the commands on separate lines. The possible commands are:

Command	Description
prog *string*	Searches the database for a string (series of characters)—this is the one command you really need to know
path *mailaddress*	Sends the output to the specified address instead of in a return message to you
site *name*	Only searches the database for the named computer instead of all available computers
compress	Compresses the output. Only use this if you expect the output to be very long.
list *string*	Returns a list of all the computers in the database that match the string. If you don't include the string, all sites are listed.
servers	Sends back a list of all the available archie servers.

Command	Description
whatis *subject*	Returns an associated entry from the whatis database, a small database that has definitions used in some files.
help	Sends back information on using the mail server.
quit	An optional command to put at the end of your list.

Doing an Archie Search by Telnet

Most archie servers also allow you to connect to them through the telnet program. This method is slow, wastes Internet resources, and, by tying up the server, prevents others from submitting their requests.

To use NetCruiser to connect to an archie server through telnet, start a telnet session and type the archie address in the Site box (Table 5.2). At the login prompt, type **archie** and then press ↵. If you are prompted to enter a password, just press ↵.

You are then prompted for commands. The commands you give at the prompt are similar to the commands in the previous section on mailing to an archie server. Typing **quit** exits the telnet program and returns you to your host computer. You can also use *bye* or *exit* to quit.

FTP is a great way to exhaust every byte of hard disk space on your computer. Through NetCruiser's uploading abilities, you can contribute to the Internet as well, and the Net works best when it's a two-way street, with people giving as well as taking. In the next two chapters you can read about the gopher and World Wide Web tools, both of which make it even easier to download specific files. Only FTP itself, however, lets you upload as well as download and gives you full access to hundreds of anonymous FTP sites.

6

Dances with Gopher

Ease of use is the war-cry, buzzword, and occasionally also hallmark of the software world in the 1990s (to mix some metaphors). Inexpensive hardware and the Windows and Mac graphical interfaces have in fact made it possible for you to do more with your PC, with less learning and greater efficiency. The Internet's getting easier too, and tools such as *gopher* are making it possible for you to concentrate on the job at hand—finding information—rather than worrying about *where* the information is located and *how* it is retrieved. You no longer have to be a nerd to explore the Internet.

NetCruiser brings additional ease of use to gopher's built-in transparency. Its gopher "client," which connects you to gopher "servers" throughout the world, can make it easier to browse diverse resources anywhere. This chapter tells you a little about what sort of beast the gopher is, a little more about NetCruiser's easy-to-use gopher program, and even more about the kinds of resources available to you using gopher. At the end you'll be able to keep up with the exponential—practically Malthusian— increase in gophers on the Internet.

What Is Gopher?

Gopher is a simple menu-driven program that makes finding information much easier than in older programs such as FTP. The menus may remind you of the menu-driven software of the mid-80s, but they are preferable to the still-used FTP and telnet Unix interfaces of the 1970s. Here are some of gopher's advantages:

Directory Trees Are Shown as Lists To choose a file to view or transfer, you do not need to type its name; you just click on it. In NetCruiser you can always tell where you are by the pointing-finger icon to the left of a menu entry. Menus can contain other menus, but if you ever take a wrong turn in a gopher burrow you can return to the previous menu level by clicking on the big left-pointing triangle in the upper right of the gopher window.

Lists Are Presented in Plain English Menus do not correspond to the static, terse directories of DOS or Unix. Instead, a menu's name usually

Gopher's Astonishing Background

Gopher was developed in April 1991 by the University of Minnesota Microcomputer, Workstation, Networks Center. Where did the name come from? The U of M football team's nickname is the Golden Gophers (goes the story). Go-fers are also the industrious college students who do their professors' library work. Gopher is a little of both—Internet mascot and hardworking go-fer. It has since grown into an industrial-strength tool for retrieving resources, used around the world. There are currently about 1500 gopher servers registered with either "Gopher Central," the University of Minnesota, or its European counterpart, but there's a total of about 5,000 gopher servers in the world—many institutions register one gopher but run several, all accessed through the registered one, and not all gophers are registered. Mark McCahill and the good people behind the gopher enterprise can be reached via e-mail at gopher@boombox.micro.umn.edu, or via paper mail at Internet Gopher Developers; 100 Union St. SE #190; Minneapolis, MN 55455, USA.

describes in plain English (including spaces between words) the information you will receive or the action that will happen if you click on it (see Figure 6.1).

Gopher Can Link to Other Tools An entry on a gopher menu can point to resources accessed in the background by Internet tools such as FTP. Again, you don't have to know the mechanics of these tools, and when you're done with your remote session you return to the gopher site from which you started.

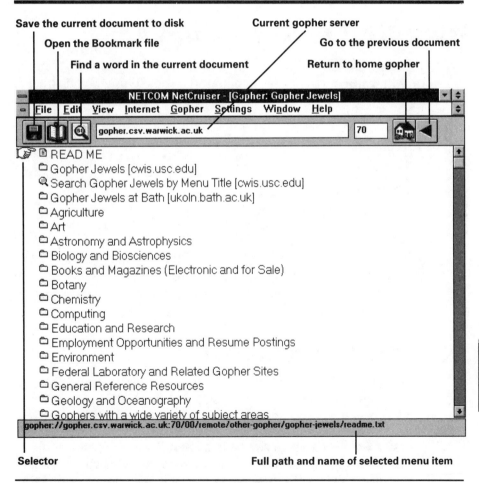

FIGURE 6.1: A sample gopher menu

The NetCruiser Gopher Clients Are Customizable When you find a place that you think you will return to, you store a *bookmark* pointing to that location so that next time you can go directly to it and not traverse menus. You'll quickly learn the most interesting gopher sites, for your purposes, as well as the sites that have the densest links to other useful sites.

Searches Are Easy Veronica is the search tool provided at many gopher sites. You enter key words, and veronica searches its database of the combined menus of all gophers for matches. See "Using Veronica" later for more about this utility.

● Using NetCruiser's Gopher

NetCruiser provides you with a gopher *client*, which is able to communicate with gopher *servers* anywhere in the world. To use it, you either select Internet ➤ Gopher - Browser or click on the gopher button on the toolbar:

There's a Usenet newsgroup devoted to gopher: comp. infosystems.gopher. Gopher discussion also takes place on the mailing list gopher-news. To subscribe, send an English-language message to gopher-news-request@boombox. micro.umn.edu.

How You Find a Gopher

When you start gopher, you'll see the Internet Site Chooser—the same map you might be familiar with if you have used NetCruiser's FTP or telnet tools. You travel to a gopher server, or site, in several ways.

Type the Gopher's Address in the Host Box A typical gopher address is marvel.loc.gov (Library of Congress). Note its characteristic domain-name style, with the elements separated by periods (sometimes called dots). Keep the port 70 (the default, or preset, value), unless you know that the port is something other than 70. Press ↵ to go to the gopher you've entered.

Use NetCruiser's Internet Site Chooser If you know the state a site's in, you can select the site by clicking on the state, then selecting the site from the drop-down list. These lists are based on the University of Minnesota's lists, but may not always take account of new gophers or gophers affiliated with official gophers.

Use Bookmarks A bookmark is a custom list of the gopher menus you use frequently. You'll learn how to keep bookmarks in the "Keeping Your Place with Bookmarks" section. It's a good idea to keep the top-level gopher you most frequently use in the bookmark file. For me, this is the all-gophers-in-the-U.S. menu at gopher.tc.umn.edu.

A subject-oriented guide, such as Rice University's (rice-info.rice.edu), is another good candidate for inclusion in your bookmark file. It can help you find information about a particular subject. This method is only as good as the list of subjects, which can be arbitrarily defined and incompletely linked to resources.

Gopher Menus: What's Inside?

Choosing a gopher menu item usually takes you to one of two kinds of information: information about information (another menu); or real information (a text or graphics file). From a gopher menu you can also open a query window or visit an FTP site. The icon next to a menu item gives you a good idea about the type of information you'll find there. Here are the common icons:

Folder The folder icon leads to another menu. Note that folders always appear closed; you can see only one menu at a time.

Document The document icon tells you that choosing the menu item takes you to text you can read; if you want you can save a copy to your hard disk by pressing the toolbar's Disk icon and specifying a name and directory on your system. Here's the Document icon:

 You can adjust the appearance of documents and directory text by fiddling with their font size, type, and style. Select Settings ➤ Gopher Options, and click on the Directory or Document button. Make your changes, and exit.

Magnifying Glass This icon opens a query window; you'll see this icon by the Veronica entry on gopher menus (Veronica is the gopher search tool).

Graphics File This icon accompanies a graphics file (.GIF, .JPG, or .BMP). If you want to download it, see the steps in "Saving a Graphics File on Your Hard Disk" a little later.

Binary File A binary file can be anything from a zipped, or compressed, file, to games software, to any executable program you might find on an FTP site accessed by gopher. A binary file on a gopher menu has its own icon:

To download a binary file, double-click the icon, then, in the Save As box, give the file a name and directory.

Saving a Document on Your Hard Disk

When you view a text document on your computer, you can choose to *keep* it there by clicking on the Disk icon on your gopher toolbar.

In the Options dialog box (select Settings ➤ Gopher Options...), you can specify the directory in which you want to save text. Image and other files you download using gopher are saved in this directory as well.

Saving a Graphics File on Your Hard Disk

You can download (get a copy of) a .GIF, .JPEG, or .BMP file in several ways. The easiest way is to double-click on the file. A Save As box comes up, where you can give the file a name and assign it a directory. Alternatively, you can download a graphics file by selecting it and choosing Gopher ➤ Download..., then completing the Save As dialog box.

Viewing What You Download To view a file, select File ➤ View Graphics File... or ➤ View Text File. Select the type of file in the List Files of Type drop-down box, then select the file name, directory, and drive using the appropriate boxes.

Double click the little box in the upper left corner of the View window when you are done. Unlike FTP, you can't download a file in gopher, then view it without saving it to a local disk.

Keeping Your Place with Bookmarks

Keeping bookmarks lets you create your own gopher-style list of the menus you use frequently, to avoid the work of remembering gopher addresses or traversing a dozen menus to go to your favorite gopher watering holes. This is a way of bringing together in one place a set of menus belonging to many gophers, located anywhere in the world.

As you move around gopherspace, you'll notice that the computer name in the Site, or address, box changes frequently. If you keep track of these computers' names and port numbers, you can in the future jump directly to one of them by adding the address to your bookmark list.

Creating a Bookmark

To create a bookmark, follow these steps:

1. Go to the gopher menu you want to use frequently by typing its address in the Site box or selecting it from the Site browser.

2. Select Gopher ➤ Bookmark or click the Bookmark icon:

3. The Bookmark dialog box comes up (Figure 6.2), with the menu name selected. If you want to use the actual menu name in your bookmark list, click Add. Otherwise, enter a new name in the Name Field. Click Done.

Gopher menus are occasionally long-winded and non-descriptive, so it's a good idea to call the menu something short that corresponds to how you think of its contents.

Using a Bookmark To go to a bookmark you have saved, just open the Bookmark dialog box, select the gopher menu you want, and click on Jump.

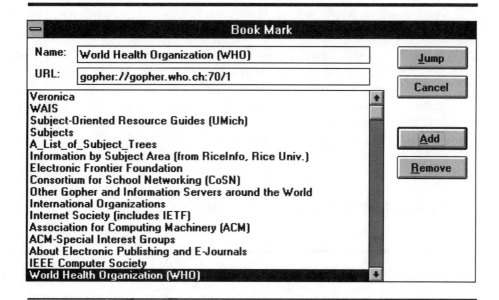

FIGURE 6.2: The Book Mark dialog box

You'll notice that under the Name field in the Book Mark dialog box is a URL (Uniform Resource Locator) field. You needn't be concerned about URLs while using gopher, since the gopher's computer name (gopher.eff.org, for instance) suffices as an address. But URLs do become important in the World Wide Web, as you will see in the next chapter.

Managing Your Bookmarks

To delete a bookmark, click on the Bookmark icon. In the Book Mark dialog box, select any bookmark you want to get rid of, then click the Remove button. For your actions to take effect, click the Update button.

Using Veronica

Veronica is not Archie's girl friend, but the Internet's Very Easy Rodent-Oriented Net-wide Index to Computerized Archives. Veronica lets you do a keyword search of either gopher *menus* or actual *document content* (the latter is called *gopherspace*). Veronica is the archie of gopherspace: a utility for identifying the location of specific gopher resources.

To use veronica, go to the gopher at the University of Nevada at Reno (where veronica was created), futique.scs.unr.edu (see Figure 6.3). You'll also find pointers to veronica on hundreds of top and second-level gopher menus, including Netcom's. The sites listed on the veronica menu contain databases of gopher menu titles and pointers to gopher documents. Choosing to search *gopherspace* gives you the opportunity to search through actual gopher documents and zero in on the documents you are seeking. In choosing which veronica to query—all veronica sites are essentially the same, in that they query the same database of menu titles—try to choose the one closest to your location to avoid unnecessary traffic on the Net.

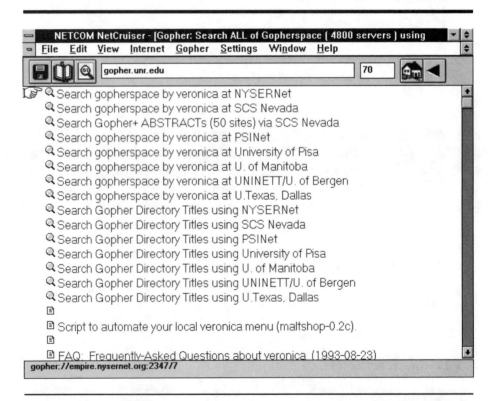

FIGURE 6.3: The veronica menu—most search sites listed here (NYSERnet, PSInet, etc.) offer you a choice between searching menu titles and searching the actual content of gopher documents (gopherspace).

Make sure to create a bookmark for the veronica server of your choice.

Here are some guidelines in using veronica:

◆ Veronica searches are not case-sensitive; veronica sees only letters, not whether they are big or small (*gopher* and *Gopher* are the same).

◆ Veronica matches only full words (searching for *net* won't return Netcom).

◆ You can restrict your search by adding *not*, as in "birds not canaries." In your veronica searches you can string together keywords using *and* and *or*. Bear in mind that searches for complicated "strings" (series of characters) can take a long time.

Everything on the Internet is subject to change. These guidelines are no guarantee that veronica will always function in this way. Chances are it will be refined and new servers will relieve the great pressure now placed on the few veronica servers.

If, for example, you want to search gopherspace for Internet statistics, you would enter something like what's shown in the top of Figure 6.4, which returns the entries shown in the bottom of the figure.

Veronica goes beyond archie in that it can bring to you the gopher menus it locates. Clicking a veronica response *takes* you to a gopher.

Navigating Gopherspace

The Unix version of gopher with which you might be familiar gives you great flexibility, but also more options than most mortals can remember.

Dances with Gopher

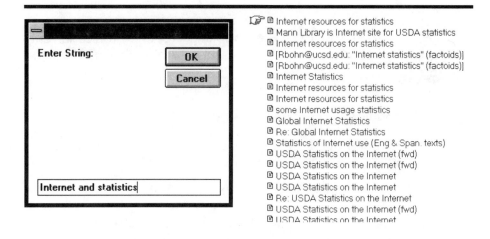

FIGURE 6.4: A veronica search (left), using Boolean string (internet and statistics), and its results (right)

NetCruiser makes it easier. In gopher, you navigate using the following techniques:

Use this...	...to do this.
↑ and ↓	Move up and down a line at a time (in menus)
→	Selects item to which finger icon is pointing (in menus)
←	Returns you to previous menu (in menu or document)
PageUp and PageDown	Move up and down a window at a time (in documents or menus)
Scroll bar	Drag the elevator window to the approximate place you are seeking in the document; click above or below the elevator window to move half a window or so at a time, forward or backward (in menu or document)

Using Gopher's Toolbar to Get Around

While using gopher you'll see the following icons to the right of the box at which you enter a gopher address:

Clicking the Home icon returns you to the gopher you initially chose by using the State lists in the Site Chooser, entering an address in the Host box, or jumping to a bookmark. Home saves you the work of traversing menus.

 To return to the Site browser to choose a **different** home, click on the Gopher icon or select Internet ➤ Gopher - Browser. As in Web, in gopher you can only have one home at a time.

Clicking the big leftward-pointing triangle takes you up a level of menus. Clicking on the Stop sign cancels an attempt to move up or down a level, or to open a gopher text document, or to transfer a file. Click Stop if no data is being transferred (the status line will tell you that 0 bytes are being transferred). The site may be unavailable or the file much bigger than you expected. Try again later.

Finding Your Way

In extra long menus (such as the list of the world's gophers, currently with about 1500 entries) or long text documents, you can track down the information you're seeking by clicking on the Find icon:

In the Find dialog box, enter the words or parts of words you are seeking, and click OK. If the text is found, the line containing it becomes the first line on your screen. If nothing is found, a message tells you the string wasn't found. To look for the next occurrence of the text, press F3. Just click OK.

Quitting Gopher

As in any Windows program, you quit gopher and return to NetCruiser's main window by double-clicking the Control menu in the upper left corner of the gopher window. Be careful not to double-click NetCruiser's Control menu; this ends your Internet session.

Gopher Gems and How You Get to Them

The following sections look at a handful of interesting gopher resources, and are randomly selected from hundreds of possibilities. Table 6.1 provides addresses for the sites you can read about below, plus some more addresses you can explore.

TABLE 6.1: Gopher Dens Worth a Visit

GOPHER SITE	WHAT YOU'LL FIND
marvel.loc.gov	Library of Congress, with pointers to governmental gophers, reference resources, copyright information, the LOC's online library catalog LOCIS, other Internet resources, etc.
gopher.tc.umn.edu	All the world's gophers, by continent and country
gopher.well.sf.ca.us	Zines, schools, politics, Big Issues of the Internet
cwis.usc.edu	Home of the Gopher Jewels, guides to subject guides

TABLE 6.1:   Gopher Dens Worth a Visit (continued)

GOPHER SITE	WHAT YOU'LL FIND
liberty.uc.wlu.edu	Washington & Lee University, with new telnet and gopher sites and other goodies under "Explore Internet Resources"
nic.merit.edu, rs. internic.net, ietf.cnri. reston.va.us	Places to go if you have Internet questions
spinaltap. micro.umn.edu	Gopher center; recipes, goodies
libra.arch.umich.edu	The University of Michigan's School of Architecture gopher; Kandinsky images
gopher.cic.net, in-formns.k12.umn.us, k12.ucs.umass.edu	K–12 resources
gopher.austin. unimelb.edu.au	Time, everywhere
ashpool.micro. umn.edu, wx.at-mos.uiuc.edu	Weather, everywhere
gopher.uoregon.edu	Lane Net, Oregon
ericir.syr.edu	ERIC: questions and answers about all aspects of education, of interest to teachers and parents
dartcms1. dartmouth.edu	Federal jobs; Dante Project
chronicle.merit.edu	Academic jobs
una.hh.lib.umich.edu	University of Michigan's rich subject-oriented guides
sunsite.unc.edu	Sun Microsystems and University of North Carolina bring you—everything
info.umd.edu	U.S. Census excerpts

TABLE 6.1: Gopher Dens Worth a Visit (continued)

GOPHER SITE	WHAT YOU'LL FIND
wiretap.spies.com	A mixed bag, from electronic books to governmental documents; fun to browse when you have nothing better to do
garnet.msen.com	Look for your next job here
gopher.netcom.com	Netcom's general-purpose gopher; abundant links to the world
goldmine.cde.ca.gov, gopher.mde. state.mi.us	California, Michigan Department of Education gophers
iitf.doc.gov	Blueprints for the National Information Infrastructure
riceinfo.rice.info	Organization of gopher and other Internet resources by subject (and links to other organizations by subject)
gopher.house/ senate.gov	House of Representatives and Senate gophers (directories, committee info, and the like—type either **house** or **senate**, not both)
rsl.ox.ac.uk	Bodleian Library, Oxford, site of high-quality graphics files
gopher.unt.edu	Gopher of the University of North Texas, with some great images from the Dallas Museum of Art's collection
library.cpl.org	Cleveland Public Library gopher, with a great reference section and model subject-oriented set of menu choices
gopher.cicnet.net	In addition to its holdings of electronic serials, an intelligent guide to Internet resources and discovery tools
athena.ifs.hr	Things Croatian

There's a somewhat dog-eared resource on the Internet called Gopher Jewels (cwis.usc.edu). It's a good place to start if you want to jump right in and start exploring. If you know exactly what you are looking for, start your explorations of gopherspace using veronica. If you know where you are looking for something, use the Internet Site Chooser.

Keeping Track of New Gopher Holes

Gophers are a fruitful breed, but Washington & Lee's gopher (Lexington, Virginia) can help you keep track of the new ones. Use your NetCruiser client to log on to the gopher (liberty.uc.wlu.edu), and follow the path Explore Internet Resources ➤ New Internet Sites ➤ New Gopher Sites. More than 400 gophers came online in one month in early 1994, including ones in Tasmania (Australia), Brazil, Krakow, and Japan.

However long it seems, the list of "All the Gophers in the World," which originates in Minnesota (gopher.tc.umn.edu) and is available from gopher servers at many sites, is not complete; it consists only of registered gophers.

Using Gopher to Learn More about the Internet

One thing the Internet lacks is a Help menu or an F1 key for a "context-sensitive" explanation of what's going on at any moment. There's no absence of documents *about* the Internet, however, and the beauty of gopher is that it can bring together geographically scattered resources in one menu. The Merit Network at the University of Michigan (nic.merit.edu) is a good place to turn when you have questions about the Internet. From the top level choose Introducing the Internet to bring up a menu of about a dozen introductory texts, including the "Internet User's Glossary." One of the things you'll find at Merit, if you dig a little, is statistics of the Internet.

Another good source of information about the Internet is the Internet Society's gopher in Virginia, ietf.cnri.reston.va.us.

Recipes

The University of Minnesota, home of the gopher, is the site where another Internet institution developed: online recipes. From NetCruiser's gopher window (the map) you get there by entering spinaltap.micro.umn.edu.

The gopher organizes recipes by food type (Appetizers to Veggies), allows you to do searches (my search for recipes with avocados turned up 20 of them), and gives you Usenet articles (with an index) culled mostly from the archives of the rec.food.recipes Usenet newsgroup.

These recipes were meant to be shared. To use them you can save them to your disk, paste them into a word-processing document, and print them out or create a cookbook.

Bringing Some Art to the Desktop

Perhaps you've heard that Microsoft now sells a CD-ROM with images and descriptions of the paintings of the National Gallery in London. If digital art is your taste, you'll be glad to know that you don't have to pay for it. Several museums, and doubtless many more in the future, are putting samples of their holdings online. For example, the Dallas Museum of Art opened an online gallery in early 1994. It provides not only superb images, but also the software you need to view them (for those without the benefit of NetCruiser). The address is gopher.unt.edu, but you can also follow this menu path starting at UMN's *All the gophers in the world*:

North America

U.S.

Texas

University of North Texas

Denton, Dallas & Fort Worth Information Services

Dallas Museum of Art - Information and Images

Museum Galleries (Images)

Digital Image Viewers

Museum of the Americas, Museum of Europe, or Museum of Contemporary Art

Select a painting you'd like to download (see Figure 6.5).

The Bodleian Library, Oxford (rsl.ox.ac.uk), is also putting art online. Choose Bodleian Library ➤ Images from the Bodleian Library. The image labels are not very helpful. 15.gif, for example, is a .gif file showing a page from a Flemish Book of Hours, ca. 1360. If your tastes in painting run to the contemporary, check out the Kandinsky Image Archive at the University of Michigan's libra.arch.umich.edu gopher; the 256-color images take up about 250K apiece.

 Veronica can help you track down images to your liking. On the Web, hypertext art galleries are coming into being, so you can view art on screen and learn about it as well. See Chapter 7.

FIGURE 6.5:   Art from the Dallas Museum of Art: Edward Hopper's **Lighthouse Hill**

What Time Is It in Singapore? Is It Raining in Des Moines?

The Cleveland Public Library (library.cpl.org) has been active on the Internet for years, being involved in the Cleveland Free-net, an Internet institution. The reference section of this library's gopher is organized by subject (Literature, Business, etc.), and offers you a useful central point of reference to begin many an exploration, and a worthy entry on any bookmark list.

What time is it in Singapore? Choose General Reference from the top level of the CPL gopher, then Local Times around the World ➤ Local time in

Singapore or wherever. This gopher is linked to servers around the world, from which it is updated frequently. Some of the "time hosts" are synchronized, and are accurate to within a second. The project of bringing together the world's local times was initiated at the University of Melbourne, Australia (gopher.austin.unimelb.edu.au).

To get the weather forecast anywhere in the United States, courtesy of the National Weather Service, go to the University of Minnesota's gopher, ashpool.micro.umn.edu (Weather). Choose a state and a city. At the bottom of the hierarchy is the information you're seeking: the current temperature, and so on, plus an extended forecast.

A great compendium of weather information is wx.atmos.uiuc.edu, the University of Illinois' "Weather Machine." This gopher includes voluminous data on the current weather and historical case studies of *all* the meteorological conditions surrounding such disasters as the great fire in California in 1993 (see Figure 6.6) and the Storm of the Century.

Another way of getting time and current weather information is via the LIBS database. Telnet to nessie.cc.wwu.edu. Log in as **LIBS**. Choose Databases and Information Services and follow the menus and prompts. You can read about LIBS in Chapter 4.

Everything under the Sun

Sunsite, an FTP/Web/gopher repository run by Sun Microsystems and operated out of the University of North Carolina at Chapel Hill, is one of the busiest gopher servers because it's one of the best. Its address is sunsite.unc.edu. It offers a wealth of information about Sun's workstation and software products:

◆ Product announcements

◆ Archived messages from newsgroups

◆ Technical white papers

Dances with Gopher

FIGURE 6.6: California on fire. A satellite view of fire plumes created by the Malibu fire of 1993.

◆ Software patches

◆ Solaris drivers

This gopher site offers a folder (menu), *Surf the Net!*, offering you access, via gopher, to other Internet tools. You'll also find good subject oriented guides.

Anytime someone has taken the trouble to organize Internet resources "by subject," you should have a look at the results. Traditionally, Internet resources were not organized at all, or were organized by the tool that could retrieve them. Subject-orientation adds real value, but is also a challenge to implement. To see some attempts at subject orientation, go to gopher cwis.usc.edu (University of Southern California) ➤ Other Gophers and Information Resources ➤ Gopher Jewels ➤ A List of Gophers with Subject Trees. Organization by subject is one of the great enterprises on the World Wide Web as well—also with mixed results. Lou Rosenfeld and Joe Janes, professors of Library Science at the University of Michigan, have done a heroic task in bringing together more than 70 Subject-Oriented Guides on subjects from law to magic, each written by someone who has plumbed the Internet for resources about a particular subject. Each Guide is further divided by subtopic, and for each resource under a subtopic you learn how it is retrieved (gopher, Usenet, whatever) and what is of interest about it.

Other folders are stuffed with resources. Strongly recommended for newcomers to the Net is *Worlds of Sunsite—by Subject*, with the subjects ranging from the Supreme Court to Welsh language and culture.

The One-Room, Red-Brick, Wired Schoolhouse

Kids in isolated rural villages will one day be able to browse the Library of Congress electronically to learn about dinosaurs and outer space—that is the vision of some supporters of the National Information Infrastructure. A grass-roots movement in state and county school districts is in fact making this vision a piecemeal reality. Lane Net, in Oregon, is one of a small number of local school districts that have their own gopher (or use someone else's—in this case, the University of Oregon's, gopher.uoregon.edu) and have begun to learn via cyberspace. These school districts' gophers are linked to each other's gophers, and ultimately to all gopher resources around the world. As a result, there is a wealth of information for teachers and parents online (see Figure 6.7).

Lane Net, a project of the Lane Service Education District and 16 Oregon school districts, reaches about 3,000 teachers and 50,000 students, as well as the millions of people on the Internet. Lane Net's aim is to provide every student and teacher with access to the Internet and to the instructional resources available online.

FIGURE 6.7: Rhododendron lovers will have to imagine the colors here—one image from the hundreds available at Harvard's Biology Image Archive gopher, courtesy of the Arnold Arboretum of Harvard Universtiy.

The Lane Net gopher offers teachers and students the following resources:

◆ Lesson plans and suggestions from teachers elsewhere. For example, an Oregon teacher using Lane Net can draw on hundreds of lesson plans that originated in Montana's Big Sky Telegraph (an Internet-linked BBS) and the Columbia Education Center, a consortium of teachers in 14 western states. Math teachers in Lane County can get some ideas for ways to teach base 4, pi, factoring large numbers, and Roman numerals.

◆ Lane Net also acts as a local bulletin board, carrying information about events at the local planetarium, and more.

◆ The Projects and Contests menu includes information about worldwide essay and chain–story-writing projects, as well as about pen-pals (a perennial favorite, online).

◆ Finally, Lane Net's gopher offers abundant information about the Internet itself, especially about resources likely to interest teachers—distance learning, the Consortium for School Networking (CoSN), e-mail lists for educators, and statewide K–12 networks.

Here are some general-purpose K–12 gophers of interest to teachers:

◆ CNIDR's Global Schoolhouse (vinca.cnidr.org), with a focus on information about space, weather, and the environment. CNIDR is the Center for Networking Information Discovery and Retrieval, a pioneering developer of Internet tools, based in North Carolina.

◆ The University of Massachusetts K–12 gopher (k12.ucs.umass.edu), a dense and valuable tangle of links to educational gophers, lesson plans, thousands of .gif images, and more. The Best of K–12 menu, from this gopher's top level, takes you to a list of dozens of other gophers, loaded with materials for kids and teachers.

While I was writing this, the California Department of Education's gopher at goldmine.cde.ca.gov and the Michigan Department of Education's gopher at gopher.mde.state.mi.us came online. K–12 is one of the hot areas of Internet expansion. There is a compendium of K–12 resources in SYBEX's forthcoming **Internet (and more) for Kids**.

A big collection of lesson plans is available at AskERIC's gopher, ericir.syr.edu. The path is Full Text ➤ Lessons ➤ Plans. Some educators consider the Language Arts lesson plans among the best available online.

The Consortium of School Networking (CoSN) gopher, digital.cosn.org, has pointers to all the state and district networks, and maintains lists of individual teachers active in networking.

Magazines Available Online

Why do print publishers put magazines online? For some, especially the publishers of the alternative Zines, information should be as free as water, and should be given away (if it's going to change the world). For others it's a way of increasing paid circulation, on the assumption that no one likes to read unformatted plain text on the computer; what's online will entice, then hook nonsubscribers. For all, putting copy online buys exposure on one of the world's hottest media. Whatever publishers' motives, for readers the result is more and more to read online—if you can put up with the computer display.

Here is a somewhat arbitrarily selected sampling of online magazines you can read without a subscription, culled from the alphabetical gopher listing maintained by CICnet (Ann Arbor) at gopher.cic.net:

◆ For AIDS researchers and activists, there are *AIDS Alert*, *AIDS Daily Summary*, *AIDS News*, *AIDS Treatment News*

◆ For humanists, the *Bryn Mawr Classical Review* and *Bryn Mawr Medieval Review*; the *Chronicles of Higher Education*; and Berkeley-based *Leonardo*, with its cutting-edge musings about society and culture

◆ For the computer-obsessed, the publications and journals of the ACM; the *Artificial Intelligence Journal*; the *Computer Professionals for Social Responsibility Newsletter*; *EFFECTOR*, published by the Electronic Frontier Foundation; *Microsoft Systems Journal*; *Windows Online Review* and *Windows Programming*; and journals dedicated to older technologies such as the Amiga

◆ For historians, *American Academy of Research Historians of Medieval Spain; CLIONET* (for historians of Australia); *Economic History Newsletter; World Heritage*

◆ Then there are the magazines you could buy at the newsstand (some only excerpted): *Wired, Mondo 2000, New Republic, New Yorker, The Economist*

The Zine Scene

The liveliest area of Internet publishing is the Zine scene. A Zine is an alternative magazine, often obsessed by the possibilities of cyberspace and radical politics of one sort or another, and targeted at a young audience.

Here are some choice Zines, available at gopher.well.sf.ca.us in Sausalito, wiretap.spies.com in Cupertino, and gopher.cic.net in Ann Arbor:

◆ Factsheet Five Electric (a review of Zines—at the Well)

◆ Practical Anarchy; Arm the Spirit (revolutionary)

◆ Funhouse ("lowlife trash kultur")

◆ Unplastic News ("What you find in this issue may be ugly, gross, and icky")

◆ Blink ("encoded with subliminal hallucinogenic algorithms")

◆ Ad Busters (a quarterly devoted to breaking the "spell of advertising over our culture")

◆ Hi-Rez (the magazine of cyber-beatniks); and Grist (also has a beat ring)

◆ Phrack (for hackers)

◆ Interzine

Some Zines are published on paper as well as online; some don't see more than a couple of issues. The Well and CIC are good places to find them archived, and you'll find some at Netcom as well.

Good Books, and Free

There are probably advantages to reading texts online: you don't have to pay for them if you're cheap, you can count the frequency with which certain words are used if you're so inclined, and you can make literature freely available to the everyone if, again, you're so inclined.

Electronic Books at the Internet Wiretap (wiretap.spies.com) currently has more than 150 titles, including Ambrose Bierce's *Devil's Dictionary*; Bram Stoker's *Dracula*; Charles Darwin's *Voyage of the Beagle*; the Bible and the Book of Mormon; works by Frank Baum and Lewis Carroll, and much more. Three dozen or so titles are available at spinaltap.micro.umn.edu, including all 302 Aesop's Fables and the complete works of Shakespeare, including the Sonnets.

Finding a Job

You are unlikely to find a job online, but it's not a bad way to learn about skills in demand in certain parts of the country or to become familiar with the way in which jobs will be posted in the future.

For information about federal jobs, try Dartmouth's gopher, dartcms1.dartmouth.edu.

Academics can learn about openings from the Chronicle of Higher Education's gopher, chronicle.merit.edu.

You can even distribute your resume to the world by uploading it to the Online Career Center database, garnet.msen.com. Visit the gopher to learn the details.

Advice for the Financially Perplexed

Messages stockpiled and archived in many Usenet newsgroups and mailing lists sometimes get buried in gopher holes. The advantage to archiving mail messages is that the material can be compiled into useful, sometimes searchable digests, for use as a reference.

One useful digest of this kind is the FAQ (Frequently Asked Questions) file, misc.invest, available at one of the great sites for FAQs, the University of Illinois at Champaign (gopher.uiuc.edu). From UIUC's top level, choose Computer Documentation, Software, and Information ➤ Usenet FAQs… and Newgroups ➤ All FAQs… ➤ Search all FAQs. The misc.invest list can enlighten you about everything from buying stocks to shorting stocks. Of course, once you do your homework and understand the basics, there's no substitute for going on Usenet or a mailing list to find answers to your own questions as they arise.

The Personal Finance guide at the University of Michigan's gopher, una.hh.lib.umich.edu, provides text information relating to Personal Finance that's available via Usenet newsgroups, anonymous FTP, as well as by gopher. You'll quickly discover that although the material is well dissected, there are only a few central sources of such information, one of which is misc.invest.faq.

Write Your Elected Official

If you don't have a job and don't invest in stocks, perhaps you should complain to someone powerful. You could post a note to Bill Clinton at

`president@whitehouse.gov`

but you'll have to settle for a written reply and a form letter at that.

To find out the phone and fax number, plus address, of your Congressional representative go to the Library of Congress's gopher, marvel.loc.gov. Choose U.S. Congress ➤ Congressional Directories ➤ Search Phone and Fax Directories for Congress. In the dialog box, type the name of the congressperson you're trying to track down. Or, you can go directly to the House or Senate gophers, at gopher.house/senate.gov (type in either **house** or **senate**, not both).

Government documents in great abundance are available online at wiretap.spies.com, including the text of the North American Free Trade Agreement (NAFTA), Clinton's economic plan, plus White House press releases, executive orders, remarks, and so on. If you're going to the beach, don't forget to take along a copy of the U.S. budget, available at sunsite.unc.edu.

Census data can be had at gopher.census.gov or info.umd.edu, or you can explore the following path, which offers some interesting detours along the Beltway: Library of Congress (marvel.loc.gov) ➤ Federal Government Information ➤ Federal Information Resources ➤ Information by Agency ➤ Executive Branch ➤ Commerce Department ➤ 1990 census. The information available here is organized by state, and is excerpted from the voluminous data of the actual census.

The U.S. Census Bureau now has a page on the World Wide Web as well. Its address is http://www.census.gov/. You can read about Web and Web addresses (URLs) in the next chapter.

If you want to know what your elected officials are doing on behalf of the Internet and the National Information Infrastructure, have a look at the new official gopher devoted to the information superhighway, iitf.doc.gov, a compilation of documents of the Federal government's Information Highway Task Force.

● Traveling, the Real Kind

If the Internet hasn't destroyed your taste for planetary travel other than by the phone lines, resources available by gopher can help you with your planning. Some of these resources have been conveniently brought together as a Rice University subject guide (riceinfo.rice.edu), under Travel. Here are some of the things you can find there:

◆ If you're traveling to one of the world's many dangerous places, you should first consult the Department of State's Travel Advisories. For every country you'll learn about entry requirements, medical facilities in the country, and terrorism (whether to worry about it). See Figure 6.8.

◆ Toll-free numbers for all major airlines

◆ Avalanche warnings, if you're heading for Colorado

◆ The archives, with a search utility, of the mailing list devoted to eco-tourism, green.travel@conf.igc.apc.org, with a year's worth of answers to questions about travel

Bosnia-Hercegovina - Warning
June 12, 1992

Although the U.S. Government recognized the independence of
Bosnia-Hercegovina on April 7, 1992, the Department of State
continues to warn U.S. citizens not to travel to Bosnia-Hercegovina
at this time because of widespread fighting throughout the country.
The Department of State strongly recommends that U.S. citizens in
Bosnia-Hercegovina consider leaving the country as soon as safely
possible. A state of war resulting in deaths, destruction, food
shortages and travel disruptions affecting roads, airports and
railways make travel anywhere in the country extremely hazardous.
In particular, the Department of State advises against travel to
Sarajevo, Mostar and the religious shrine at Medjugorje, all of
which are located in areas which have seen heavy fighting.
Travelers should be aware that the U.S. recently suspended
operations of the Yugoslavian national airline, JAT, in the United
States.

FIGURE 6.8: State Department Travel Advisories can advise you of countries to avoid.
Here's the first warning of trouble in Bosnia-Hercegovina.

◆ The University of Manitoba's Travel Information Library, a valuable
collection of links to other gophers

Going to Croatia?

Media super-hype about the information superhighway has made the Internet seem like an after-hours hangout, a prototype for the network that
will bless us with video on demand. In the real world, the Internet is a
priceless form of communication (and occasionally, medium of public
relations) for some of the more troubled parts of the world. The gopher
athena.ifs.hr in Zagreb, Croatia provides the means for journalists of the
Zagreb Foreign Press Bureau to disseminate information about conditions
in former Yugoslavia. Press releases, daily clippings, and miscellaneous re-
portage by the Zagreb Foreign Press Bureau contain rich information
about life and war in Bosnia-Hercegovina.

For armchair travelers to Croatia (sensibly heeding the State Department's travel advisories) the gopher offers information about dozens of museums and galleries of Croatia.

 To follow events in this part of the world, you can read the articles in the Usenet newsgroup, alt.current-events.bosnia. Read the relevant clari newsgroups for newsfeeds.

Returning Home: Netcom's Gopher

Netcom's gopher (gopher.netcom.com) is a good, general-purpose gopher, loaded with menu items pointing to other gophers that are pointing to other gophers, in typical gopher fashion. If you need a gopher home, this is a fine choice. You'll get the following:

◆ Information *about* the Internet. The path Internet information ➤ Internet Assistance-Collected Resources leads you to a gold mine of documents about the Internet to help you use archie, e-mail, mailing lists, FTP, and so on.

◆ Gopher links *to* the rest of the Internet: FTP, archie, jughead (a fancy newer search utility), and various directory services.

◆ A menu of all the world's gophers (the one from Minnesota), plus veronica of course.

◆ A menu of items pointing to "government" gophers, including gophers that are supported by Federal money such as ASKEric, a great resource for educators (described in more detail in the next chapter).

◆ Internet-style odds and ends: local times around the world and today's events in history.

Gopher is a powerful tool, currently faster and easier to use even than the World Wide Web. But because of its conceptual power and sheer promise, the Web may soon threaten gopher's popularity, especially among new users of the Internet. There's no arguing with ease of use.

Web: The Best of the Net

The World Wide Web has for long been a tool of the haves of the Internet—folks with powerful workstations and direct, high-bandwidth connections. Now NetCruiser gives PC users a Web *browser*—a graphical tool for using the World Wide Web. With the NetCruiser browser you can click highlighted passages in documents and go directly to related documents. You don't need a fancy workstation any more to enjoy point-and-click access to the World Wide Web.

This chapter shows you how to make the most of NetCruiser's Windows-based graphical browser and takes you on a tour of some great Web sites. I think you'll find the Web about as exciting as the Internet gets.

 NetCruiser's Web browser is very similar to a popular program called Mosaic, software created by the National Center for Supercomputer Applications at the University of Illinois. There are versions of Mosaic for Unix XWindows, Windows, and the Macintosh. Using your NetCruiser browser, you can use the Mosaic "home page," getting the benefits of Mosaic without the technical difficulties of configuring it on your computer. Its address is provided in Table 7.1: URLs Worth a Visit, a little later in this chapter.

What Is the World Wide Web?

Remember footnotes? In a printed book a footnote tells you to flip to the bottom of the page or the end of the chapter (or book) to get information related to the text you are reading: for the source from which the text came, for an explanation of what the text means, for related information elsewhere in the book you're reading, or for the author's commentary about what you are reading. World Wide Web brings the power of footnotes to the universal library that the Internet is shaping up to be. From within documents you are reading you can, using the Web, click on highlighted words or phrases to get definitions, sources, and related documents, located anywhere in the world. Better than footnotes, Web links you to actual documents, not just references to them.

Web makes available the massive information resources of the Internet using a footnote-like technique called *hypertext*. The best way to appreciate what hypertext is all about is to compare it with the linear text of a book. A printed book imposes a beginning-to-end structure on information. You usually read a book from beginning to end, and most books are organized on the assumption that's how books are used. A reference book breaks the linear structure, but you are still forced to flip between entries because of the A–Z (linear) method of organizing. In a hypertext reference, you would click on "See Also" and go directly to the cross reference.

Hypertext was originally envisioned as a text-only system, but soon encompassed every kind of information that could be stored on a computer, including images, sound, video clips, and data tables. Current hypertext documents—**hyperdocuments**—used on PCs with CD-ROMs often contain all of these elements. Of course, anything that can be stored on disk or CD-ROM on a **closed** computer system (a system that's not networked) can also be distributed over the Internet. Several years ago HyperCard for the Macintosh tried to make the hypertext approach to information organization available to non-programmers, but never quite reached its potential.

Hyperdocuments assume that people's information needs differ. From any page of a hyperdocument about baseball, one reader will want to pursue the history of baseball, another the ways stadiums are designed, someone else will want to read about the life of Sandy Koufax, and so on.

Figure 7.1 shows a sample page from a Web page. Notice the underlined words; that's where you click.

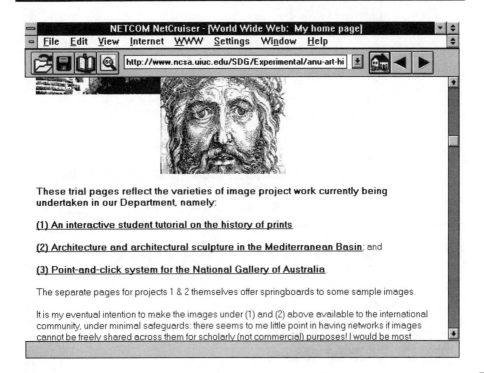

FIGURE 7.1: The starting point for a Web search, a guided tour of the history of art, created at the Australian National University

Clicking on *An interactive student tutorial on the history of prints* takes you to Figure 7.2 (top), but clicking on *Point-and-click system for the National Gallery of Australia* takes you to Figure 7.2 (bottom). The top image in

Web: The Best of the Net

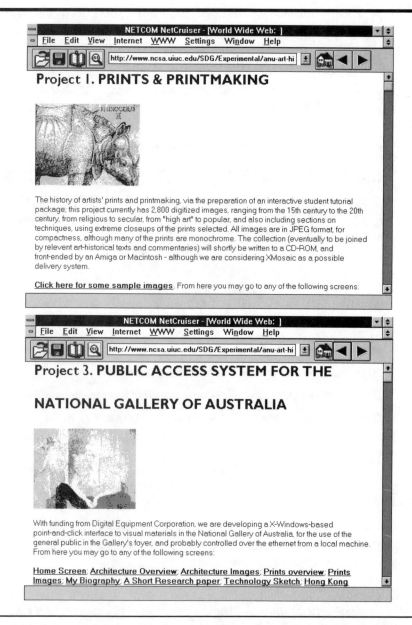

FIGURE 7.2: The first stop from Figure 7.1 for a person looking for information about the history of prints (top); the first stop from Figure 7.1 for a person looking for a guided tour of an art gallery (bottom)

Figure 7.2 contains many additional hotspots. Before long you have wandered far afield from your original starting point; or, if you are doing a search for something specific, you have zeroed in on what you are searching for, or gotten close to it.

Web and Gopher

The NetCruiser tool most like the Web is gopher, the subject of Chapter 6. (If this book were hypertext, you could click *gopher* at this point to go to a table of contents for Chapter 6 and zoom right in on anything that interested you.) Your gopher and Web tools are *front ends*: they give you an easy-to-use and consistent way of looking at information located on *back ends*, or servers. Using both gopher and Web you can use FTP (to download a file) and other Internet tools. Later you'll see this in action. In Net-Cruiser, the gopher and Web interfaces are similar, because the code is shared.

 Like gopher, the Web is a client/server program. With Net-Cruiser you get your own Web client, which you use to connect to and use Web resources located on Web servers. A little later you will see how to connect to a Web server in Switzerland that lists all the Web servers in the world, organized by country.

What's different is the way Web and gopher organize the resources they make accessible. Gopher imposes a hierarchical organization on information—a series of nested menus (menus leading to other menus, ultimately leading to something useful, maybe). The structure of the menus and the wording of the choices is arbitrary, as well as hierarchical: You have to interpret someone else's menu names (some say "surfing" the Internet, while others say "cruising"), and if what you are searching lies at the bottom of a hierarchy of ten menus, you must climb down every rung of the ladder. (Of course, you can create a bookmark or do a veronica search, but the structure of the information *requires* that you use these time-saving tools.)

In Web, information is not organized in a hierarchy but in—a web. You decide where you want to go, and you go there directly. As in gopher, with NetCruiser you can keep bookmarks to speed up access once you've identified useful sites.

In Web you will encounter menus of links, but the closer you get to real information (text and images), the more links are embedded in documents that provide a context in which to interpret and evaluate them.

Using the World Wide Web (or gopher) to retrieve information helps reduce the amount of traffic on the Internet. When you access a document using NetCruiser's Web browser, the document is transferred to your host computer and the link is broken. This prevents the Web server from having to hold open a line while you read the document. By including direct links in the document, a Web document prevents readers from having to constantly run FTP to retrieve ancillary documents.

 A link is called an **anchor** in the language of the Web.

It's Not Perfect

Web is wonderful in concept, but not perfect in the real world of cyberspace. In using Web you depend on links selected by others and crafted to facilitate travel from resource to resource. Any two people will choose different passages to link, different documents to link *to*, and the links will never be as comprehensive as you would like; there's simply too much *stuff* out there on the Internet.

It's also easy to lose your way in the Web, because the comforting order of gopher menus is missing. Bookmarks and a history file that keeps track of every link you've traversed are not just helpful, but indispensable, in Web.

Finally, when you move from document to document, you are transferring more data to your computer than if you just bring down a set of gopher menu names, which is all you do in gopher most of the time. This is especially true because with your Web browser you see in-line graphics; these files are *big*.

On balance, Web is more fun than gopher, but its performance is more sluggish, especially if you are doing something like downloading satellite images from Australia.

More than any other NetCruiser tool, the Web browser requires a pretty powerful computer and a fast modem.

The World of URLs: Web Addresses

In the Web, documents are linked to other documents. A *link* is called a *Uniform Resource Locator* (URL), and looks like this: **http://www.ncsa.uiuc.edu/General/NCSAHome.html**. This is what's known as the *home page* for Mosaic, a graphical browser. You'll see a lot of such links when you use the Web, and you need to be comfortable with what they mean. *http* stands for *hypertext transmission protocol*, and indicates that the link is to a document on a Web server. Instead of http you might see *file*, *gopher*, or *FTP*, which means the link takes you to file (either local or on an anonymous FTP site) or to a gopher server. After the double slashes (//), you see a computer address (www.ncsa.uiuc.edu, in this case), a directory path *at* that address, and the document in question, in the directory path. The document you are linking *to* in this case has an extension, .html, which means hypertext markup language and is shortened to .htm in Windows. When you keep bookmarks in NetCruiser, you are keeping a list of URLs. When you use the navigation keys to move to the next and previous documents you've used, NetCruiser can do this because it has kept track of the URLs you have visited. And of course, you can type a URL directly into the Web browser to jump directly to a Web document you've never seen before and haven't recorded in a bookmark. For more information about making Web pages yourself, use Web to go to http://www.ncsa.uiuc.edu/demoweb/html-primer.html. This document about *hypertext* is itself a hypertext document with many links to other documents.

Using NetCruiser

To start your Web browser you either select Internet ➤ World Wide Web (never has the Internet been simpler!) or click on the Web button:

The Web browser window is shown in Figure 7.3.

You can remove your toolbar by clicking on View ➤ Toolbar to see as much of a Web document as possible.

When you use the Web, you'll notice a new menu on your menu bar. The WWW menu duplicates the functions of the tools on the Web toolbar. In addition, Settings ➤ WWW Options… gives you considerable control over how your browser looks, as you'll see in a later section on customizing your Web.

Getting Around

The basic unit in the Web is the *page*, a (usually) text-plus-graphics document with links to other pages. Navigating means, primarily, moving around from page to page. A page in the Web is a dynamic document.

The most important page is your *home page*: the page your browser opens to when you start a session, and the page you jump to, during your wanderings, when you click the Home button (see Figure 7.4).

As you move your mouse across a page, the URLs (see the sidebar on URLs) of clickable hotspots—links to other pages—appear in the status line at the bottom of the window. Your customary mouse icon (an arrow pointing to the upper left) turns into a straight-up arrow whenever you pass over a link.

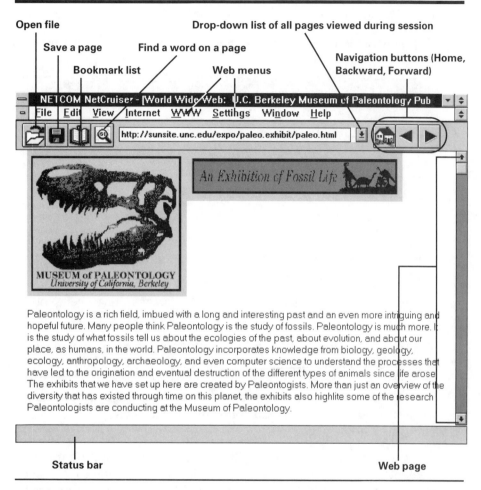

Open file

Save a page

Bookmark list

Find a word on a page

Web menus

Drop-down list of all pages viewed during session

Navigation buttons (Home, Backward, Forward)

NETCOM NetCruiser - [World Wide Web: U.C. Berkeley Museum of Paleontology Pub

File   Edit   View   Internet   WWW   Settings   Window   Help

http://sunsite.unc.edu/expo/paleo.exhibit/paleo.html

An Exhibition of Fossil Life

MUSEUM of PALEONTOLOGY
University of California, Berkeley

Paleontology is a rich field, imbued with a long and interesting past and an even more intriguing and hopeful future. Many people think Paleontology is the study of fossils. Paleontology is much more. It is the study of what fossils tell us about the ecologies of the past, about evolution, and about our place, as humans, in the world. Paleontology incorporates knowledge from biology, geology, ecology, anthropology, archaeology, and even computer science to understand the processes that have led to the origination and eventual destruction of the different types of animals since life arose. The exhibits that we have set up here are created by Paleontogists. More than just an overview of the diversity that has existed through time on this planet, the exhibits also highlite some of the research Paleontologists are conducting at the Museum of Paleontology.

Status bar

Web page

FIGURE 7.3:   This is your World Wide Web control center. The buttons give you the power to create and jump to bookmarks, to save a Web document on your own hard disk, and to navigate the Web with point-and-click ease.

See "Customizing the Way Your Web Looks" for procedures for changing the way a page, a link, and a mouse icon **look** in NetCruiser.

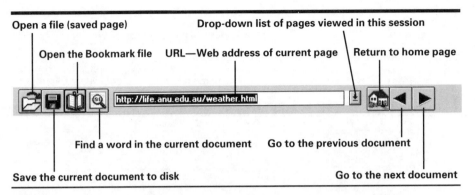

FIGURE 7.4: The Web toolbar's navigation buttons

Ordinarily you navigate the Web by clicking on underlined text. When you do this, a connection is made and data for the page transferred to your computer. This can take a while.

If you want to backtrack or revisit a page where you have been, you can move around using either the WWW menu or the Web toolbar.

The Forward button (WWW ➤ Forward) takes you to the next page—the page your cursor is pointing to if it's on a link. The Back button (WWW ➤ Backward) takes you to the previous page. The Home button (WWW ➤ Home) takes you to the page you can choose as the default starting point for your Web sessions. See "Customizing the Way Your Web Looks," on choosing a home page.

To go to a page whose address (URL) you know, but that is neither on your bookmark list nor on the list of all the places you've been to during this session, first get rid of the current page's URL in the text box on the toolbar. Just select it using your mouse and press ↵ to delete it. Then enter the entire URL you want to use, and press ↵.

History—URLs You Have Visited

Choosing WWW ➤ History... brings up a dialog box showing all the pages you've used in a session. You can jump to any link in your travels by selecting it and clicking Jump.

The drop-down list box in NetCruiser's Web toolbar also shows you the path (including all your backtracking) from your home page to your current page. Click the down arrow to see a list of links you've used. Use this list to jump to a page you saw several links ago.

Using Bookmarks

Bookmarks keep track of the Web sites you like to visit. At any point you can get to the Bookmark dialog box by either selecting WWW ➤ Bookmark... or clicking on the icon showing an open book:

From the Bookmark dialog box (see Figure 7.5) either jump to a site whose address you have already stored (select it and press Jump) or save a new address (just press the Add button). Click Done or press Esc when you're done.

Book Mark	
Name: Bill's Lighthouse Getaway	**Jump**
URL: http://gopher.lib.utk.edu: 70/0/Other-Internet-Resource	**Cancel**

MTV
Sunsite based Multimedia exhibits and expositions
United States Geological Survey-HTTP Server-Home Page
Internet Distribution Services
OTIS' links to other art things
Mosaic home page
ncsa home page
The World-Wide Web Virtual Library: Subject Catalogue
Data sources classified by access protocol
An Internet Hypertext List (6/16/93)
 Telemedia, Networks, and Systems Group
multimedia index (from MIT)
Bill's Lighthouse Getaway

Add
Remove

FIGURE 7.5: The Bookmark dialog box

You can prune your list of bookmarks by removing ones you don't use; just select a link and click Remove. Clicking Done returns you to the Web.

When you add a bookmark to your list, you can give it a meaningful name. In the Name field you can edit NetCruiser's choice of a plain-English name so that it means something to you (NetCruiser's choice is usually pretty good, though). URL addresses themselves are pretty intimidating-looking, and are meant to help computers, not people, find resources.

Finding Data on a Page

If, in the Web, you are primarily concerned with text documents, it can be handy to search text for a specific word or words (this is sort of like searching gopherspace using veronica). Just click on the Magnifying glass tool (see Figure 7.4), complete the Find dialog box, and click OK.

The longer the document, the more useful this tool. The list of the world's HTTP sites almost requires that you use the Find tool to find a place where you know there is a great Web server (such as the United States Geological Survey page).

A Find query shows you the line with the first instance of the word or characters you are seeking, and makes that line the first (top) line of your display. To find the next instance, press F3. If the word or words don't appear in the document, you'll see a message. Click OK or press Esc.

Saving and Opening Files— Why You Want to Do It

NetCruiser gives you the means to easily keep a copy of any page you want to use as a home page, by selecting File ➤ Save or clicking on the Save icon, which shows the picture of a disk (Windows' conventional Save icon—see Figure 7.4). Page files can be big, and usually contain the coding for the links. To switch to a saved page, select File ➤ Open WWW File or click on the Folder button and select a saved page. To make a saved page your *home* page, see "Choosing a Home Page," below.

Saving and studying pages as text documents in your word processor is a good way of learning how the hypertext markup language, HTML, works.

Downloading an Image File (GIF or JPEG)

The status bar shows a URL with a .gif or .jpg extension or something similar if your mouse is pointing at an image file. To download the file, select WWW ➤ Load to Disk. Then click on the file you want to download. In the Save As dialog box, give the file a name and directory, then click on OK.

NetCruiser does not yet let you download an inline graphic—an image used as illustration or decoration on a page.

Customizing the Way Your Web Browser Looks

NetCruiser gives you much choice in displaying pages the way you want. Tinker with your settings until your browser display looks best and is most legible for you. You customize your Web display by selecting Settings ➤ WWW Options..., and using the Options dialog box. The box offers you three sets of choices: General, View, and Fonts, each available by pressing a button on the left of the dialog box. See the three dialog boxes in Figure 7.6.

Choosing a Home Page (Options/General)

The home page is your point of reference when you use Web. You should try to choose a home page that is the most effective nerve center for the sort of work you do; if you explore, use Netcom's default home page, or

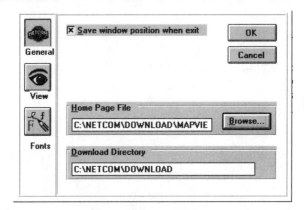

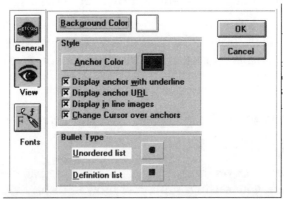

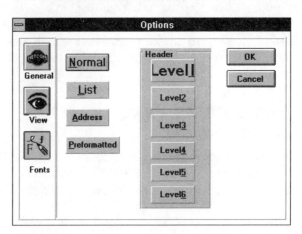

FIGURE 7.6: Use Settings ➤ WWW Options to bring up this set of three dialog boxes (click on one of the three buttons to the left to see a different box).

the Mosaic or CERN home pages (see Table 7.1, later in this chapter). By saving pages (which you do by clicking on the Save icon) you can build up a set of home pages from which to do your exploring. Pages you save are automatically stored in the Download Directory specified in the Options box. You specify a home page using the Home Page File field. To search for a page in another directory from the default (Download Directory), click on Browse, navigate your directories, and select a page of your choice.

Changing Background Color If You Get Bored with White (Options/View) Click on the Background Color box to bring up a Windows palette from which you can select a color for your display. Unfortunately, you can't choose the color of the text, so make sure any background you choose retains the legibility of the text.

Changing How Your Links Look (Options/View)

When you click on the View button of the Options box you get a set of Style options. The wording of these options is somewhat opaque, but they all have to do with links, or *anchors* as they are called here. The options let you (in order)

◆ remove the underlining of anchors (links). To change the anchor's color, click Anchor Color, make a selection, and click OK.

◆ choose to display or not display the URL in the status bar (the URL can be distracting to people with sensitive peripheral vision or annoying if there are many links).

◆ display or not display in-line graphics files (displaying them can slow down performance).

◆ turn off the special link cursor (the big upward-pointing arrow) if you don't like it (it is distracting, and if you can see the address in the status bar you already know that your cursor is on a hotspot).

You can also make more cosmetic changes, such as defining different bullets for unordered and definitional lists by clicking on the appropriate buttons; numbered lists use numerals, of course. See the next section for more information on lists.

Changing Fonts (Options/Fonts)

The hypertext markup language requires that documents be formatted in levels and that lists be coded. The elements of an HTML page include ordered lists, unordered lists, and definitional (descriptive) lists. A definitional list has two elements: a name, such as *National Center for Supercomputing Applications*, and a description, such as *The NCSA is located on the campus of the University of Illinois-Champaign.*

You can customize how the headers and lists of a Web document look by changing their font type, size, and style (bold, italics, normal), taking advantage of the fact that every Web document is highly formatted to begin with. This is a great feature for people who have trouble reading the computer screen or want to emphasize or de-emphasize certain parts of pages. If your eyesight is good, smaller type lets you see more on a page and compensate for the S-L-O-W rate at which the page scrolls.

Quitting Web

To quit the Web browser, choose File ➤ Exit or double-click the Control menu in the upper left of the window (the little box). Clicking on the big box takes you out of NetCruiser.

Pearls of the Web

It's the nature of the Web that no two people will pursue the same path of links; they will start and end at different places; even if they start and end at the same pages, they will take different routes along the way (not a bad metaphor for the Internet as a whole, actually). Here are some suggestions for starting your explorations. From these sites you can go just about anywhere. Most of the links mentioned in the rest of this chapter (and a couple that aren't) are provided for your convenience in Table 7.1.

Using Web to Learn about Web

As with every Internet tool, Web is the best place to start if you want to learn about the Web. If you start a Web session from Netcom's home page

TABLE 7.1:   URLs Worth a Visit

URL	WHAT YOU'LL FIND
http://www.ncsa.edu/ SDG/Software/Mosaic /NCSAMosaicHome. html	The Mosaic home page
http://www.ncsa.uiuc. edu/demoweb/html-primer.html	This hypertext markup language primer (organized as hypertext, of course) is available at the National Center for Supercomputer Applications, in Illinois
http://www.ncsa.uiuc. edu/General/NCSA-Home.html	The NCSA's home page
http://info.cern.ch/ default.html	Start here to search the Web by (1) subject (2) site or (3) type of service (FTP, etc.), a good home page
http://www.cis.ohio-state.edu/hypertext /faq/usenet/top.html	Just the FAQs, about everything; a hypertext list of most of the known FAQs
http://www.ncsa.uiuc. edu/SDG/Software /Mosaic/Docs/whats-new.html	A great place to see a list and description of new Web servers, in the current month and by day. At the end of this long list are hotspots that will take you to listings of new servers for previous months.
http://cui_www.unige. ch/OSG/MultiMe-diaInfo/index.html	High-power locus of multimedia information and files, with archived FAQs and Media Archives (links to huge image, sound, and video archives) in Switzerland
http://www.wired.com/	Full-text, searchable archives of *Wired* magazine, homage to the digital revolution
http://life.anu.edu.au/	All you wanted to know about the environment, everywhere

TABLE 7.1: URLs Worth a Visit

URL	WHAT YOU'LL FIND
http://info.cern.ch/ Space/Overview.html	A wealth of information for teachers, parents, and anyone who loves the skies; all the NASA centers are here, plus BBS's for skywatchers, lists of companies, the American Astronomical Society home page, and more
http://www.ksc.nasa. gov/ksc.html	Kennedy Space Center, NASA, information about current and historical space missions
http://hypatia.gsfc. nasa.gov/NASA_home page.html, nasa_hot-tipics.html	NASA's home page, takes you to hotspots (for the public), all NASA centers, and subjects; itself not very interesting
http://hillside.coled. umn.edu/	Hillside Elementary School, Cottage Grove, Minnesota, Web server
http://web.cal.msu.edu /JSRI/GR/grintro.html	Grand River, Michigan, Elementary School Web server
http://eryx.syr.edu	AskERIC, for teachers; digests of information about curriculum, the schools, the world of online education resources, searchable, to boot
http://unite.tisl.ukans. edu/xmintro.html	The home page for the Explorer, a Web browser designed for kids in school; dozens of lesson plans are available here
http://uu-gna.mit. edu:8001/uu-gna/ index.html	Usenet University/Global Network Academy's home page, with links explaining how an online university might work
http://www.cs.wash-ington.edu/research/ community-net-works/	Links to more than two dozen community freenets

TABLE 7.1: URLs Worth a Visit

URL	WHAT YOU'LL FIND
http://info.er.usgs.gov/	Audio and visual displays about the U.S. Geological Survey; information about GIS's—Geographical Information Systems; press releases from National Earthquake Information Center; history of the USGS, other goodies
http://legowww.itek.norut.no/	LEGO blocks: their history, some project ideas, .jpeg images, a tour of a LEGO factory, and more, from Norway
http://www.cm.cf.ac.uk/	The movie database server in Cardiff, Wales
http://www.census.gov/	The U.S. Census bureau's census page
http://white.nosc.mil/images.html	A great compendium of images and sounds, well selected and well organized; particularly good on the European sites
http://www.ncsa.uiuc.edu/SDG/Experimental/anu-art-history/home.html	The start of a hypertext history of art; one of the Net's best efforts to inform, enlighten, and entertain at the same time
http://cui_www.unige.ch/w3catalog	An excellent home page: preliminary efforts to devise an archie-like or veronica-like search utility for the Web; provides links to Yanoff's list, CERN's subject list, NCSA's what's-new list, and much more. Another place that's worth watching closely.

and want to learn about Web, proceed to http://info.cern.ch/hypertext /WWW/Provider/Overview.html. (If you don't find a clickable hotspot, type this URL into the Browser's text box.) Here you'll find an excellent primer about hypertext and the hypertext markup language, and you will get some general advice for setting up your own server and creating your own links. Another good source, for people who want to learn HTML or set up their own Web Server, is http://oneworld.wa.com/htmldev /devpage/dev-page.html.

CERN: The Center of the Web

CERN, the high-energy physics lab in Geneva, Switzerland, and home of the World Wide Web initiative, has a home page known to all Web fans, http://info.cern.ch/default.html. The home page informs you that there is no "top" to the Web, but belies this modesty by offering you three extremely useful central listings of Web servers:

Save a copy of this page to your hard disk, so you can use it as your home page. At least include it in your bookmark list.

Choice	Comments
Virtual Library by Subject	Mostly pretty academic. However, from here you can link to other subject lists, which give you richer but more idiosyncratic and less reliable lists.
List of servers	By country, alphabetically. Very useful if you know where your server is. Use the Find utility to look for a site; otherwise, navigation of long Web documents such as this one can be a pain.
by Service Type	Lists of, and links to, FTP, gopher, telnet, etc., sites. The easy way to use FTP and WAIS; the hard way to use Usenet news and gopher.

The current version of NetCruiser supports links only to FTP and gopher. More are planned.

Subject Guides to the Web

The Virtual Library subject catalog has an academic slant and is not comprehensive. Other subject listings are available by choosing *other subject catalogs of network information* from the top level of CERN. This is a profoundly browsable collection of subject-oriented guides, including the Subject-Oriented Guides from the University of Michigan.

If you search enough, you will encounter numerous attempts to impose some grand scheme on the Web (such as the University of Brussel's Principia Cybernetica Project). Such projects tend to collapse on themselves: developing a scheme for "all knowledge" is a lot easier than finding the knowledge on the Internet to plug into the scheme. CERN's "by subject" list remains a pretty good place to start any Web expedition.

If information on a Web server seems old, look for a place to click called **What's New**. Look there for recent updates to the server. The ultimate What's new for the World Wide Web is available at http://www.ncsa.uiuc.edu/SDG/Software/Mosaic /Docs/whats-new.html. You'll find here the newest Web servers, including ones that aren't registered at CERN and so don't show up on one of CERN's lists (by service, subject, place). At the very end of this long list you will find links to What's New lists for previous months. This is a great way to see where the action is on the Web. You can also see a list of all new Web sites using gopher: at liberty.uc.wlu.edu go to Explore New Internet Sites ➤ New WWW sites.

Multimedia

The strands of the Web are a perfect channel for distributing multimedia data (audio, video, animation, image, and text files), if you have the network bandwidth and computing horsepower. A nexus of information about this subject is brought together at MIT's Telemedia, Networks, and Systems group (http://tns-www.lcs.mit.edu/tns-www-home.html).

From MIT you can link to the Index to Multimedia Information Sources in Switzerland and the Multimedia Laboratory in Boston. Both contain archives of multimedia files plus information you can read on screen about the latest thing—MIDI, mpeg, mbone, whatever. In Switzerland, there is a useful archive of relevant FAQs on audioformats, CDROMs, image processing, and so on. The Media Archive has links to a huge number of image, sound, video files. The Swiss URL is provided in Table 7.1.

Some Web displays are dynamic: They show continuously changing video images or keep track of users or some other number that changes from time to time. To refresh your display and see the latest images or information, select WWW ➤ Reload.

For a museum-style multimedia exhibition (roller coaster pictures, Dr. Fun, the Underground Music Archive), turn to the following page: http://Sunsite.unc.edu/exhibits/exex.html.

Wired Magazine

Wired Magazine makes for a good read, even if you don't believe that digital technology is changing the world beyond recognition and for the better. Now the entire magazine is available in hypertext (Web) format, at http://www.wired.com/. Articles are searchable, and you have a chance to read some of the best writers of the digital revolution. What you miss reading *Wired* online is the magazine's innovative design, perfectly suited to its subject and point of view. *Wired* is also, of course, an excellent way to keep current about the Internet.

Internet World is also available online—in excerpts and via gopher—at gopher.internet.com. This magazine is both more practical and less portentous than Wired, so the two magazines complement each other well.

NASA

Despite what you read in *Wired* or your newspaper, real space is still a lot more interesting than cyberspace. There's no better source of current information about space programs than the Web servers run by NASA. NASA's home page (http://hypatia.gsfc.nasa.gov/NASA_homepage.html) is a convenient gateway to the rich resources of NASA. You can explore NASA by subject (aeronautics, biological sciences, computers, social sciences) or by NASA institution (Johnson Space Center, Ames Research Center, Kennedy Space Center, the Washington, D.C. headquarters, and so on). There is material here for scientists, students, K–12 teachers, and the curious. The space images have great intrinsic interest, and are good PR for NASA.

CERN has a Space page with comprehensive links to world sites, including NASA: http://info.cern.ch/Space/Overview.html.

The educational resources are particularly rich. From NASA Web pages, you can connect to the JPL educator's guide (an FTP site with images and documents of interest to parents and teachers). Kennedy Space Center (http://www.ksc.nasa.gov/ksc.html) provides historical archives with information about early astronauts and missions, as well as a huge manual, completely rendered in hypertext, that can be used to learn about the current space shuttle program. You can download a catalog of NASA's Space and Earth Science Data CD-ROMs, some containing databases of images.

The Langley Research Center High Performance Computing and Communications Program makes some of NASA's computing resources available to schools, part of their bigger effort to strengthen math and science education in the U.S. One teacher for each of several selected school districts in Virginia has received training, and several high schools are now using NASA computers via their own Macs to do simulations and data analysis in physics classes. NASA provides the Sun computers and direct Internet connections the schools need.

NASA also makes available a wealth of images of galactic goings-on. The Planetary Data System archives, for example, offers images of planets, and you can download photos taken by the Hubble Space Craft, before and after it was repaired (see Figure 7.7). Beyond this, happy browsing; NASA makes some great material available to the curious public (like the Hubble photos at URL: http://hypatia.gsfc.nasa.gov/hst/wfpcII_pr.html).

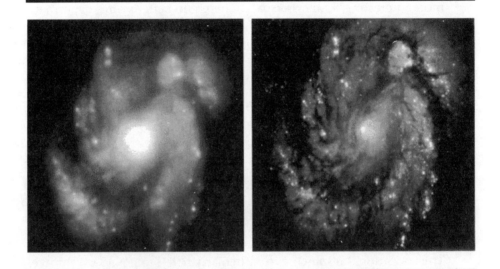

FIGURE 7.7: Before and after—photos of the M100 galaxy before and after the repair of the Hubble Space Craft, courtesy of NASA's Jet Propulsion Laboratory (JPL)

Australia, Web Hub

The Australian National University (ANU, an acronym you will see all over the Internet) is a prodigiously rich source of information about weather and the natural environment generally, and not just for Australia. Links from ANU take you to weather servers around the world, via FTP, telnet, gopher. The URL is http://life.anu.edu.au/.

This is the site for:

◆ Current weather satellite images of every part of the world (see Figure 7.8).

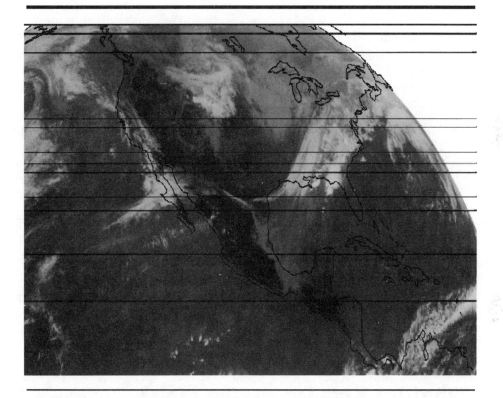

FIGURE 7.8: An infrared weather map of the U.S., courtesy of the Australian National University data banks

◆ Biology, medicine, neuroscience, landscape ecology resources.

◆ The Web server for FireNet, an international bulletin-board service (BBS) for fire-management specialists, with a tremendous amount of information about how fires start, spread, and stop; software for simulating fires; and bibliographies; there is information here about the Listserv mailing list and the FTP site dedicated to fires.

◆ Up-to-date earthquake information. Internet people seem to be pre-occupied with earthquakes.

The First Elementary School with a World Wide Web Server

In March 1994 the world's first and second Web servers in *elementary schools* were set up. The first was Brad Marshall's fifth-grade class in Grand River, Michigan. The kids in Mr. Marshall's class went online to find pen-pals and to do some online science experiments with other kids. To attract a pen-pal every kid in the class provided a personal sketch, complete with favorite color, hobby, movie, and subject.

The world's second Web server in an elementary school was Mrs. Collins' sixth-grade class of Hillside Elementary School in Cottage Grove, Minnesota, which is working with the University of Minnesota College of Education to make use of Internet resources in the curriculum. Both class Webs include photos of the kids.

The school's URLs are http://hillside.coled.umn.edu/ (a directory on the University of Minnesota's server) and http://web.cal.msu.edu/JSRI/GR/grintro.html (Grand River).

The world's first elementary school with its own **gopher** was the Ralph Bunche School on West 123rd Street in New York City (ralphbunche.rbs.edu; part of Bolt Beranek and Newman's NSF-funded National School Network Testbed).

What Do Kids Do on the Web?

Much of the promise of the Web is just that, for now. But because kids like to look at screens and school districts are often strapped to *buy* resources, the lure of the Net is great, at least in schools that can afford the computers and connections. The beauty of the Internet is that kids don't have to wait for resources to come to them; they can create their own resources. As the kids in Minnesota and Michigan are discovering, they *are* the resources. Here are some other things they can do on the Internet. (The "NASA" section, earlier, gives an additional sampling of a few of the great NASA resources for kids and teachers.)

AskERIC

ERIC, the Educational Resources Information Center, is a federally funded educational resource for teachers, based at Syracuse University. AskERIC, an Internet institution, is an e-mail based "question-answering" service for teachers that is also of interest to parents; ERIC staff answers questions on just about anything of interest to teachers. Famous for years as a telnet and gopher site, AskERIC has recently come to the Web.

AskERIC's home page, http://eryx.syr.edu, is organized like a library—exactly the right metaphor—with a virtual main desk, librarian, reference section, and stacks (the virtual library proper). There are lesson plans, bibliographies, addresses of mailing groups for the entire K–12 curriculum. The virtual reference section includes searchable reference dictionaries and a gateway to related educational materials, such as the Department of Education's Web and gopher servers. In the "stacks" you can read through a dozen or so archived mailing groups (Listservs) and browse FAQs about subjects such as gun control, year-round school, distance education, home schooling, and multimedia. Great stuff here for parents, teachers, and the curious.

Field Trips

The great thing about the Web is that it strongly conveys the sense of *going places*. That's because you can see pictures from places around the world. For kids (and anybody) who like to travel or learn, or both, there are good destinations coming online almost every day. For starters, there's Australian National University's art-history exhibit (Figure 7.1) and Berkeley's Museum of Paleontology (Figure 7.3). (The Figures show you the URL.)

Lighthouses Bill Britten has assembled photographs of historical lighthouses, with commentary, and generously made them available to the world at http://gopher.lib.utk.edu: 70/0/Other-Internet-Resources/Pictures/Lights/lights.html. These images are intrinsically relaxing, somehow, but no substitute for a real visit. See Figure 7.9.

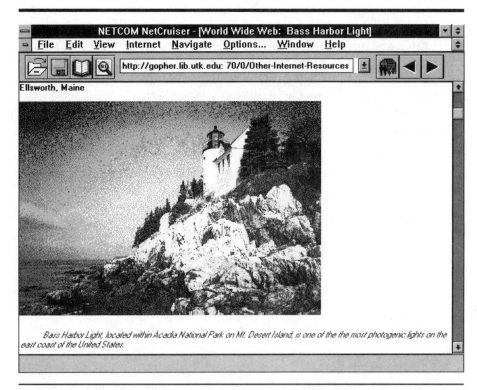

FIGURE 7.9: Bass Harbor lighthouse, Maine, part of the collection of lighthouse photos assembled and made available for the world at the University of Tennessee.

Exploratorium Kids with access to a Web can discover the Exploratorium, a superb hands-on science museum, even if they don't live in San Francisco, the museum's home. This Web server has plenty of information about membership, hours, and local programs, of course. It also attempts to bring the Exploratorium's exhibits to the kids of the world by making available dozens of .jpeg images of colored shadows, the Exploratorium's distorted room, kinetic light, the momentum machine, and other cool things. Several exhibits are re-created for the Web medium, and you can experience the visual, audio, and musical works of many of the Exploratorium's artists in residence. Maybe by the time you explore this site you will be able to read online a copy of the *Explorer*, a quarterly magazine for Exploratorium members. See Figure 7.10.

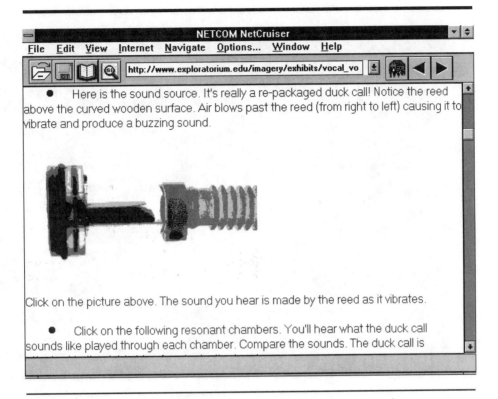

NETCOM NetCruiser

File   Edit   View   Internet   Navigate   Options...   Window   Help

http://www.exploratorium.edu/imagery/exhibits/vocal_vo

• Here is the sound source. It's really a re-packaged duck call! Notice the reed above the curved wooden surface. Air blows past the reed (from right to left) causing it to vibrate and produce a buzzing sound.

Click on the picture above. The sound you hear is made by the reed as it vibrates.

• Click on the following resonant chambers. You'll hear what the duck call sounds like played through each chamber. Compare the sounds. The duck call is

FIGURE 7.10:   One of the Exploratorium museum's cool exhibits.

Library of Congress Exhibits Sunsite (University of North Carolina) has assembled links and introductions to a series of rich Library of Congress exhibitions—on the Vatican, 1492, the Dead Sea Scrolls, and the Soviet Archives—each packed with images, original documents, and explanatory text. The Sunsite URL is http://sunsite.unc.edu/expo/ticket _office.html.

LEGO For LEGO lovers, there's a Web page in Norway with information about LEGO products, ideas for things to make, and, of course, pictures of amazing things people have built with LEGO blocks (Figure 7.11).

FIGURE 7.11: Here's a piece of LEGO sculpture inspired by the Hubble Space Craft. Created by Steve Putz at Xerox PARC, the image is available at the unofficial LEGO hangout on the Web, based in Norway. See Table 7.1 for its address.

Adult Education: Learning C++ on the Internet

The Global Network Academy, in Texas, founded in 1992, is the prototype of what might be the first accredited university on the Internet. You'll find all the trappings of a university: teacher/consultants to answer questions by e-mail, hypertextbooks, and, as library, the Internet itself, for which the GNA is in the process of creating a huge meta-index.

Unlike FTP with archie and gopher with veronica, Web has no search utility, a deficit you'll miss. You might want to look into the experimental search services, available at http://cui_www.unige.ch/W3catalog—a good home page!

Classes will take place using *MUDs* and *MOOs*, interactive programs that allow on-screen meetings, in real time.

One of the first classes offered was on C++, the object-oriented programming language. Usenet newsgroups devoted to the GNA are grouped under alt.uu.*. Check your NetCruiser newsreader and the Web page (http://uu-gna.mit.edu:8001/uu-gna/index.html). All the tools are in place to make this idea work, and if GNA makes its university successful, it can only enrich the Internet as a whole. (Soon there would have to be online classes for Internet beginners.)

The Web's Future

A quick scan of existing Web sites in CERN's list of registered sites gives the strong impression that the Web has been used mostly by academics, and mostly in the highly technical parts of the academic world—departments of physics, astronomy, and computing. The Web's academic character is greatest outside the U.S. A list of new Web servers shows much more of the same, but also a growing mix of non-academic organizations with their own Webs:

◆ The Bay area band, Towhead, whose home page has song demos (2 MB files), photos, and concert schedules

◆ *Inter Text*, *Mother Jones*, and *Wired* magazines

◆ An "obituary" page

◆ "Bad Subjects: Political Education for Everyday Life," based at Carnegie Mellon University's versatile English Server—browse it sometime! — at http://english-server.hss.cmu.edu

◆ A public radio station in Tennessee (WUOT)

◆ Kite flying

◆ Early instruments (microscopes mostly) at the University of Naples

◆ The two elementary school classes mentioned earlier in this chapter

◆ A Calvin and Hobbes page, for fans of the great comic strip

The Web says it all about the Internet. It is capable of encompassing all the important tools, including FTP and gopher. And the Web is capable of encompassing all resources, even though the amount of knowledge available on the Internet is pitifully small, relative to what could be available online. Take part in the Internet, and the Web will come into its own.

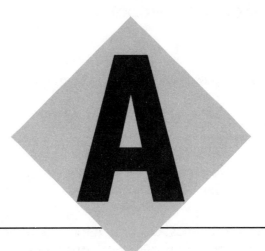

Installing and Configuring NetCruiser

Installing NetCruiser on your computer is like installing any Windows program: the Setup program prompts you for information, then informs you of the progress of the installation. When you are done you will have a computer equipped with a point-and-click Windows interface to the Internet, which makes the whole thing as easy to use as possible.

What You'll Need

To use the NetCruiser software, you'll need

- ◆ Windows 3.1 and DOS 5.0 or 6.x.
- ◆ A 386, 486, or faster computer.

You need a fairly powerful computer (386 or faster) to run *Windows* effectively. You'll also need

◆ A mouse.

◆ A modem, either external or internal.

◆ Enough space on your hard disk, about 3 MB, to hold the entire NetCruiser program.

To get the most out of NetCruiser, you should buy the fastest modem you can afford and one that supports the v.42 error-correction and V.42bis data compression technologies. If you're new to modems, you might want to read Sharon Crawford's clear and helpful introductory book, **Your First Modem** (SYBEX).

What you *don't* need is telecommunications software (such as Windows Terminal). That's because, with TCP/IP and SLIP software, you create a virtual network; instead of using telecommunications software to dial into another "host" computer, your computer becomes a working *part* of the Internet.

Just Insert the Disk and...

Getting TCP/IP and SLIP software to work together used to take a good deal of tinkering. In addition, you had to find and separately install Internet applications, or *clients*, and get everything to work together.

With NetCruiser you install the protocol and the Windows interface, as well as the individual Internet tools, *all at the same time*, just as you install any Windows program. Here's how:

1. With the NetCruiser disk in your A or B drive (whichever one takes 3½" disks), choose File ➤ Run. In the Run box, type **A:\setup** or **B:\setup**, depending on where the NetCruiser disk is. The Setup program checks your hard disk for the amount of available space. If you don't have enough space to install the program, NetCruiser will display a message recommending that you make some extra room on your computer. If you have enough space, the Welcome to NetCruiser Setup box comes up (see Figure A.1).

FIGURE A.1: You use this box to tell the Setup program where you want to install the NetCruiser files.

2. The Setup program assumes you want to create a new directory called *Netcom* and install the NetCruiser files there. If that's the case, click Continue.

Installation now starts, and the NetCruiser Setup box displays for you its progress, both in the percentage of files installed and the names of the files as they are being decompressed and installed. (NetCruiser files are compressed, so NetCruiser won't run if you copy them manually or with File Manager.)

3. When the files are installed, the Modem Settings box (see Figure A.2) comes up, asking you to tell NetCruiser the following:

◆ What type of modem you are using. If you can't find your modem on the list, choose *Generic*.

◆ How fast it is in *baud* (for all practical purposes this is the same as *bits per second*, although the two are technically different). NetCruiser uses the highest baud possible for any modem setting you select, so if you had a 14.4 (14400) modem, you'd select *19200*.

◆ The "Connector"—the communication port your modem uses. If you're not sure which communications port your modem uses, click COM2. That is the right choice for most Windows systems. If you choose the wrong one no harm will be done, but NetCruiser will not be able to complete the connection to the Internet. Thus, in the worst case, you can try each choice until one works.

Click OK to proceed to the next step.

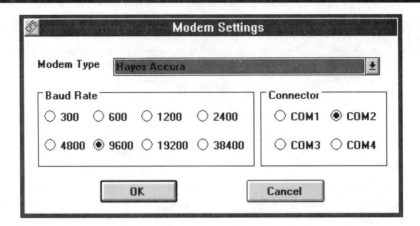

FIGURE A.2: You specify your modem type, speed, and port here. Once NetCruiser is installed, you can change these settings at any time.

4. The Phone Number box now comes up (Figure A.3, top), displaying a default (preset) phone number for your modem to use, in the Dial field. To change the number, click the Directory button. From the Choose an Access Phone Number box (Figure A.3, bottom), first select a phone number from the Phone Directory, then indicate whether you want that number to be preceded by an area code, by a 1, by a prefix such as 9 (used by many businesses for outside calls), or by some combination of these numbers. Click OK. In the Phone Number box that comes up again, confirm that the number in the Dial box is the one you want to use, and click OK.

5. If everything went OK, the NetCruiser Setup box tells you that installation is complete. Click *Start Registration* or click Exit and register later by running the NC Registration program.

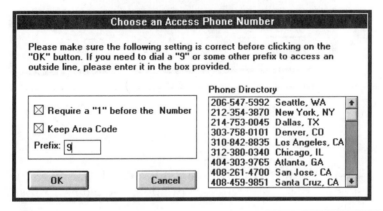

FIGURE A.3: This box (top) tells you the number your modem will use to call Netcom. You can change the number after installation using the Settings menu. Click Directory to see the window (bottom), then select a new phone number. If it's in a different area code make sure the area code and "1" boxes are checked; if your business uses a 9 for outside calls, or some other prefix, indicate that as well.

Registering with Netcom

To use NetCruiser, you must provide Netcom enough information to bill you and keep track of your account. After you have installed NetCruiser and clicked the Start Registration button, the window comes up shown in Figure A.4.

FIGURE A.4: The first window you see when you register with Netcom

1. Click OK to go to the Registration Information window (see Figure A.5). Click OK. During registration, you tell NetCruiser three things:

- ◆ Your name and address (for billing purposes)

- ◆ Credit card information (type, number, expiration date) for automatic billing

- ◆ Your *user name* and *password*

If you have questions about registering NetCruiser or **cancelling** your registration, refer to the online Help system. You do not need to run NetCruiser to use Help; just double-click the NetCruiser Help icon in NetCruiser's program group.

```
┌─────────────────────────────────────────────────────┐
│               Registration Information                │
├─────────────────────────────────────────────────────┤
│  First Name: [Ella]        Last Name: [Peal]          │
│  Address:    [2 Irving Street]                        │
│  City:       [San Francisco]    Phone: [        ]     │
│  State:  [CA]  Zip Code: [944444]                     │
│  Company:    [Ms Mops]                                │
│ ┌─ Choose Your Username and Password ──────────────┐  │
│ │ Username:      Password:     Enter the Same Pass- │  │
│ │                              word Here:           │  │
│ │ [ella]         [**********]  [**********]          │  │
│ └───────────────────────────────────────────────────┘  │
│       [ Continue ]              [ Cancel ]             │
└─────────────────────────────────────────────────────┘
```

FIGURE A.5: You use the Registration Information window to tell Netcom where you live, how you want to pay for your service, and how the system is going to recognize you (user name and password).

Your **user name** must be eight or fewer characters and begin with a character. It shouldn't include special characters. It should be meaningful to you and others, because it will form the first part of your e-mail address (see Chapter 2, "Anatomy of an Address"). By convention, user names are lowercase and based on real first or last names, or both. Your **password** should consist of six or more characters, **should** include special characters, should also both include upper- and lowercase characters, and shouldn't be guessable—avoid your name, your spouse's name, your birthday, or a word that is likely to be found in a dictionary. It's a good idea to alternate letters and numbers and lower- and uppercase characters.

2. Click Continue when you are done. You won't be able to proceed if any required fields (such as first and last name) are not filled in. The NetCruiser Registration window comes up. Enter your five-digit Registation Number, which is printed in red on the disk label. Press Continue. A modified Phone Number window (see Figure A.6) comes up. Enter a prefix, if appropriate, and click Continue.

Now click the OK button in the Registration Status window. Net-Cruiser dials an 800 number, then transmits and confirms the data you entered, to complete the registration process.

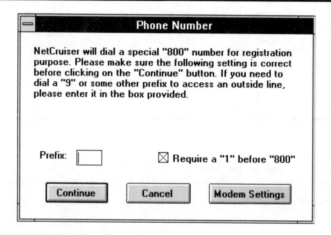

FIGURE A.6: The Phone Number window confirms the phone number you entered during installation.

3. The Registration Status window (see Figure A.7) displays for you what's going on as the information you supplied is transmitted to Netcom, validated, and stored. Next, the Billing Information window comes up, showing the billing scheme for your account: the startup fee, if any; the monthly subscription rate; and the connect fee, if any, for hours above the free hours allotted you each month. Select the type of credit card you wish to pay with and enter the card number and expiration date in the space provided. Click OK. The Terms and Conditions window comes up. Read the window *carefully,* then click OK. The Registration Status window returns and verifies your credit card data and user name. Press OK.

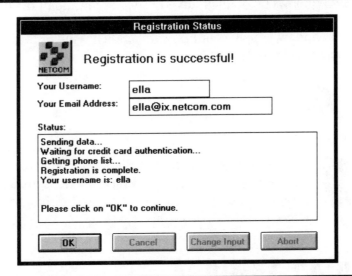

FIGURE A.7: This window tells you what's going on at each step of the registration process.

4. The Phone Number window now comes up—the same one you used during installation to choose an access number. Because the list of phone numbers on your installation program might already be out of date, the registration process downloads a list of the current local access numbers. Review the list to make sure the number you chose during installation is still the best for you. To change your access number, follow the instructions in step 4 of the preceding section. When the Welcome to NetCruiser box comes up, click OK.

User names must be unique on a host computer, so if you choose a user name already used by a Netcom subscriber, the Registration Status box recommends an alternative—the user name you recommended followed by a **1** (or a **2** if the name ended in 1, etc.). Click OK, and you will start the process over from the point at which you entered data in the Registration Information window. Confirm the selections at each step until the Registration Status window looks like Figure A.7. Click OK and you'll see the Welcome to NetCruiser box.

A new Windows program group is created at the end of the installation process. To start NetCruiser, all you do is double-click the NetCruiser icon in that window, supply your password, and click OK or press ↵. That's all it takes to get onto the Internet!

NetCruiser

 If you've followed these steps carefully and NetCruiser does not start up—or if you're having any kind of trouble with the program, see Appendix C for troubleshooting tips. You can also call Netcom at 1-408-983-1510.

● Changing Settings

Once you have installed NetCruiser, use the Settings menu to make changes in the way you have set up NetCruiser.

Changing Your Account Setup

To change any information that Netcom uses for billing purposes, click Settings ➤ Edit User Information.

1. You'll be prompted to enter your password in a dialog box. Do so and click OK. The View/Edit User Information window comes up (see Figure A.8)

2. Change your address if you want Netcom to use a different address for billing. Provide a new or different credit card type and number, with expiration date, to assign your usage charges to a different card.

3. Press OK when you're satisfied with your changes, or of course Cancel if you change your mind.

 The credit card and other personal data you enter while registering NetCruiser passes over a network owned and controlled by Netcom. No one but Netcom has access to that data.

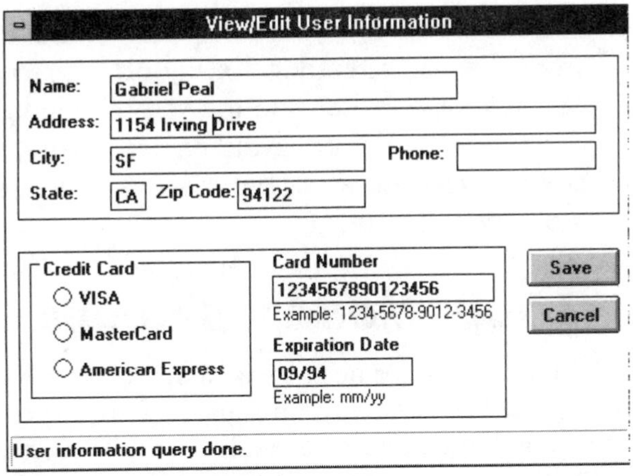

FIGURE A.8: Use the View/Edit User Information window to make any changes to the billing information Netcom maintains.

Changing Your Password

You can't be too careful on the Internet; enough people want your password for you to take some precautions. Changing your password frequently can't hurt. To do so just select Settings ➤ Change Password. In the Change Password window (see Figure A.9), type in the old and new passwords, re-entering the new one in the appropriate field to make sure that both you and the system got it straight. Click OK to accept the password, and click Cancel to close the window and return to the main window.

FIGURE A.9: Change your password frequently!

You should change your password frequently, especially if you work in an office setting. It's a good idea to use all the characters at your disposal, and to use both numbers and digits. In choosing a password, avoid names of yourself or anyone close to you and avoid birthdates and addresses. The more arbitrary, the better.

Changing Your Modem Settings

If you get a new modem or need to use a different communications port of your computer because you've installed a new device such as a printer, select Settings ➤ Modem Parameters. From the Modem Settings window (Figure A.2) select a new modem from the drop-down list (click on the downward-pointing arrow) and click on the new settings for that modem, or change the settings for the existing modem. Press OK or Cancel.

Changing Your Phone Number

If you're on the road and want to dial into a different Netcom site, or if you move, or if a Netcom site opens up across the street, you can change the phone number your modem uses to dial Netcom by selecting Settings ➤ Phone Number. First a Phone Number window comes up reminding you of the number your modem is currently using to get to a Netcom computer (Figure A.3, top).

To change that number, click Directory. From the Choose an Access Phone Number window (Figure A.3, bottom), select a number from the Phone Directory on the right, using the scroll bar as necessary. As appropriate, place check marks in the boxes to the left. A prefix is a number such as 9, which some businesses use before the 1 preceding the area code. Click OK or Cancel to return to the Phone Number window, and confirm that the Dial number is what you want (you can edit it if it's not). Press OK to confirm your choice.

Changing the Way Individual Tools Work

In addition to letting you configure NetCruiser as a whole, the software allows you to configure the way some of the individual tools work. Both gopher and Web give you an Options... dialog box, available from the menu bars for those tools, allowing you to adjust things like color and type size. See Chapters 6 and 7 for instructions for adjusting your gopher and Web settings.

Keeping NetCruiser Up to Date

A unique feature of NetCruiser software is its ability to keep itself up to date. You don't have to wrestle with shrink-wrapped boxes filled with shrink-wrapped disks, bulky documentation, and loose mailers, and you don't have to worry about the software maker losing track of you and your address if you move. The best thing is, updates are free!

Software changes for many reasons, and software that gives you mastery of the Internet is even more volatile, since the tools and protocols are improved and acquire new and more powerful features, and new tools and utilities come into existence from time to time. *Netcom is committed to constantly improving the NetCruiser software package.*

Upgrading NetCruiser Software

To upgrade your NetCruiser software, you must first establish whether Netcom has a more recent version of the software available for you to use.

1. From the main window (the one with the globe), select File ➤ Download New Version to bring up the *Download new version* window (see Figure B.1). If you have the latest version, a message window tells you so. If you don't have the latest version, the *Download new version* window displays values in the *Size of downloading files* and the *Time estimate* fields.

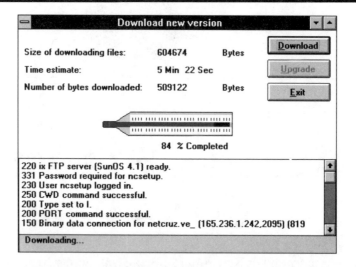

FIGURE B.1: If there is a later version of NetCruiser than the one installed on your machine, NetCruiser detects the difference and this window displays the number of bytes of new files to download and the estimated time it will take to download them.

2. To download the new files, click the Download button. The download process starts. The thermometer graphic monitors its progress in percent-completed, while the *Number of bytes downloaded* field shows you exactly how many bytes have been downloaded.

If for any reason the download process stalled, press Exit from the **Download new version** window, and try again later. If you continue having problems, close the Setup program. Phone Netcom or send e-mail (using the previous version of Net-Cruiser), as instructed at the end of this Appendix.

3. When all the files are successfully downloaded, a message informs you that everything went OK. Click OK, then click on the Upgrade button for the upgrade to take effect (the button is dimmed—unclickable—until everything is downloaded). The Setup program then prompts you for permission to close "all running sessions." Click Yes. Now you see the NetCruiser Upgrade window (see Figure B.2).

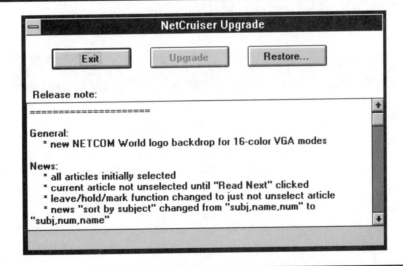

FIGURE B.2: The NetCruiser Upgrade window gives you the chance to read about the new version of the software you just upgraded, or to back out of the upgrade process (click the Restore... button) if something went wrong.

4. If things went OK and all the new files were downloaded, clicking Upgrade in the NetCruiser Upgrade window confirms your desire to install the new version of the software, saving the version you *were* using so you could restore it. Take a moment to read the description of the new version of NetCruiser in the Release note box in the bottom half of the window. Click Exit to return to Program Manager. Here's what you see:

Click OK.

5. Now, test the new version by double-clicking the NetCruiser icon and connecting to Netcom.

If You Need Help

For general and billing questions, call Netcom at 1-800-501-8649 or use the Web to read the page http://www.netcom.com/netcom/homepage.html.

For all technical questions, use the Help System or call Netcom at 1-408-983-1510.

To send e-mail to Netcom technical support, address your message to

support@netcom.com

To write Netcom a letter: Netcom Customer Services, 3031 Tisch Way, San Jose, CA 95128.

To receive the latest points of presence, call 1-800-488-2558 or use FTP to download the file /pub/netcom/access_numbers from the site ftp.netcom.com.

Helpful Hints

Remember that NetCruiser is unlike most other telecommunications software that you have used before. NetCruiser actually makes your computer an Internet node using its networking software and your modem connection. When you set it up, you might need to attend to a few details.

This appendix addresses some of the more common problems that first-time NetCruiser users might encounter when registering with NetCruiser. If you're having a problem, you'll probably find the solution here.

Problem When I run Setup, NetCruiser locks up or crashes.

Solution You may have an application or driver running that is incompatible with NetCruiser. First try closing conflicting applications, then, if that doesn't work, check the driver.

To close conflicting applications that run automatically:

1. Exit Windows, then restart it.

2. Press Ctrl+Esc to call up the Windows Task Manager. This will show you any applications that are running.

3. Close all applications except the Program Manager before installing NetCruiser.

We have had the best luck running NetCruiser with Windows' original communications driver (**comm.drv**). To check the communications driver that Windows is running:

1. Locate the **system.ini** file in the Windows directory.

2. Open the file with Windows' Notepad or another text editor and check the first section for a line that starts with *comm.drv=*. If it does not read *comm.drv= comm.drv*, edit it to *comm.drv=comm.drv*.

 Always make a backup copy of system.ini before you make any changes. Then, if something goes wrong, you can restore order using the backup copy and try again. It's a good idea always to have backup copies of important files.

Problem I received the error message *Connect Error 10014, open Com0 failed*.

Solution This error indicates that NetCruiser is unable to open the communications (COM) port selected in the modem setting screen. Either you have selected the wrong COM port or there is another application that is currently using the COM port.

1. Verify that your modem is attached to the correct COM port, or if it is an internal modem, that all switches are set correctly.

2. Close all applications before running NetCruiser Registration.

To further diagnose the problem you can use the **Terminal** application in **Accessories**. Run this application to verify that you can talk to the modem.

1. Select the *Settings* menu and then select *Communications*.

2. Select the COM port for your modem. Click OK.

3. Type AT in the terminal window and press ↵. If you are connected properly the modem should reply OK on the next line in your open terminal window. (If the modem doesn't reply OK, go back to step 2 and select a different COM port. When you've got the right COM port, you'll see the OK message.)

If your system has fax software installed, it may conflict with NetCruiser's access to the COM port. To verify that the COM port is free:

1. Close all applications that are running, but remain in Windows.

2. Double-click **Startup** in the Program Manager. Any programs displayed in Startup will automatically run when you load Windows.

3. Create a new directory and move any applications from Startup to the new directory.

4. Go to the **Windows** directory, and open the file called **win.ini**. This file contains two lines, *load=* and *run=*, that start applications when Windows is started.

5. Comment these lines out by preceding them with a semicolon (;). For example:

```
run=c:\fax.exe
```

becomes

```
;run=c:\fax.exe
```

 If this fixes your NetCruiser problem, it may be that your fax software is incompatible with NetCruiser. You won't be able to run both at the same time.

Problem Modem initialization fails.

Solution This problem can arise either when the modem is not responding to NetCruiser or if you have selected the wrong modem type.

1. Verify that the modem is powered on and connected to a good phone line.

2. Power the modem off, then on, to make sure it's completely reset.

3. Select a different modem type in Modem Settings. If your modem is not listed, try the **Hayes Accura** setting. If this fails, try the **generic** setting.

Problem NetCruiser continually says *call failed.*

Solution Again, there are two possible reasons for this error: either you are using an incorrect or bad modem cable, or you have selected the wrong modem type.

If you suspect the problem is related to the modem cable, verify that the cable connecting the modem to your PC supports pins 1–8, and 20. If it is a 9-pin connector, then all the pins need to be used. In "techno-talk," this cable needs to support full modem control and hardware flow control signaling. This particular problem can be caused by pin 8 (DCD) failing to operate.

To ensure the correct modem type selection:

1. Power the modem off, then on, to make sure it's completely reset.

2. Select a different modem type in Modem Settings. If your modem is not listed, try the **Hayes Accura** setting. If this fails, try the **generic** setting.

Problem NetCruiser Registration connects but fails in the login.

Solution This problem occurs when you have selected the wrong modem type.

1. Power the modem off, then on, to make sure it's completely reset.

2. Select a different modem type in Modem Settings. If your modem is not listed, try the **Hayes Accura** setting. If this fails, try the **generic** setting.

Problem NetCruiser Registration connects but says the modem configuration is wrong.

Solution This error can be caused by an incompatible communications driver in Windows, an incorrect or bad modem cable, or wrong modem type selection.

To check the communications driver that Windows is running:

1. Locate the **system.ini** file in the Windows directory.

2. Open the file with Windows' Notepad or another text editor and check the first section for a line that starts with *comm.drv=*. If it does not read *comm.drv= comm.drv*, edit it to *comm.drv=comm.drv*.

If you suspect the problem is related to the modem cable, verify that the cable connecting the modem to your PC supports pins 1–8, and 20. If it is a 9-pin connector, then all the pins need to be used. In "techno-talk," this cable needs to support full modem control and hardware flow control signaling. This particular problem can be caused by pin 8 (DCD) failing to operate.

To ensure the correct modem type selection:

1. Power the modem off, then on, to make sure it's completely reset.

2. Select a different modem type in Modem Settings. If your modem is not listed, try the **Hayes Accura** setting. If this fails, try the **generic** setting.

Problem When I start Registration or run NetCruiser, I get the message *threed.vbx too old*.

Solution This message appears when there are multiple copies of the file **threed.vbx** on your system.

1. Locate the file threed.vbx in the Windows directory.

2. Rename this file **threed.old**.

3. Restart Windows and run NetCruiser again.

Problem When I enter the date in the credit entry screen, NetCruiser Registration immediately says the date is incorrect.

Solution The date field uses the date format defined in the Windows Control Panel International settings.

1. Go into the Windows Control Panel and double-click on the **International Settings** icon.

2. Select the date format *mm/dd/yy*. Click OK.

3. Rerun the NetCruiser Registration program.

Problem NetCruiser generates an error message, *out of memory*.

Solution The message means either that Windows is running in Standard Mode or doesn't have enough virtual memory. To check the status of Windows:

1. Select the *Help* menu in **Program Manager**.

2. Choose the *About Windows* option.

Helping Hints

This should indicate that Windows is running in Enhanced Mode and has at least 10,000 KB of memory. If Windows is running in Standard Mode it may be because it was started with the command **win/s** or because it is run on a 286 processor. To force Windows to run in Enhanced Mode, start it with the command **win/3**.

To increase the memory available to Windows you can increase the size of the swap file in the virtual memory settings by doing the following:

1. Select **Control Panel** from the Program Manager.

2. Double-click the **386 Enhanced** icon.

3. Click on the Virtual Memory option and increase the size.

4. Restart Windows.

This will increase the memory in Windows. For more information, refer to your MS Windows documentation.

Problem NetCruiser hangs when running **Download new version**.

Solution This error is due to excessive errors in the communications with the network. Such errors can result from selecting a baud rate that exceeds the capabilities of Windows, using an incorrect type of modem cable, or choosing a wrong modem type in the Modem Settings window.

To correct errors resulting from excessive baud rates, change the baud rate in Modem Settings to 2400 baud and try downloading again. For a standard Windows setup, 19200 baud should be fine. On some PCs without high speed UARTs (serial communications port), you may need to use 9600 baud.

High-speed UARTs can be checked by running **c:\windows\msd.exe** from the DOS prompt. Enter **C** to display information about the COM ports. The last line displays the type of UART. The 16550 UARTs are the high-speed UARTs.

If you suspect the problem is related to the modem cable, verify that the cable connecting the modem to your PC supports pins 1–8, and 20. If it is a 9-pin connector, then all the pins need to be used. In "techno-talk," this cable needs to support full modem control and hardware flow control signaling. This particular problem can be caused by pin 8 (DCD) failing to operate.

To ensure the correct modem type selection:

1. Power the modem off, then on, to make sure it's completely reset.

2. Select a different modem type in Modem Settings. If your modem is not listed, try the **Hayes Accura** setting. If this fails, try the **generic** setting.

Problem NetCruiser locks up. Mouse is frozen and won't move.

Solution This can be caused by using an incompatible communications driver in Windows.

To check the communications driver in Windows:

1. Locate the **system.ini** file in the Windows directory.

2. Open the file with Windows' Notepad or another text editor and check the first section for a line that starts with *comm.drv=*. If it does not read *comm.drv= comm.drv*, edit it to *comm.drv=comm.drv*.

Problem NetCruiser says Username/Password is incorrect.

Solution Make sure you register successfully before attempting to use NetCruiser. If you have registered, make sure that the password is being entered in the same case in which it was originally created. Passwords are case sensitive, i.e. "password" is not the same as "PASSWORD,"

If you have a NETCOM host dial account and have received NetCruiser with a special registration code for NETCOM users, you may not have entered the same Username *and* password as your host dial account. In order to be eligible for this special program, and to be able to have your e-mail forwarded properly from your host dial account, you will need to use the same Username. To make certain that no other person can register your Username, you will need to register with the *same* password. After you have registered your NetCruiser account, you can use the NetCruiser Settings menu to change your password.

Helping Hints

Problem I downloaded the latest upgrade but I'm still running the same version.

Solution Take these steps:

1. Exit out of NetCruiser.

2. In Program Manager, open **NETCOM**.

3. Double-click on the icon with the word NEW and labeled Upgrade.

4. In the dialog box that opens, click on the Upgrade button.

5. After a few seconds a dialog box will appear saying the upgrade was successful. You can now run the new version of NetCruiser by double-clicking on the NetCruiser icon.

 Technical support for NetCruiser is available from Netcom at 1-408-983-1510.

Index

Note to the Reader: Throughout this index **boldfaced** page numbers indicate primary discussions of a topic. *Italicized* page numbers indicate illustrations.

TALK TO SYBEX ONLINE.

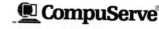

The information and power of the Internet can be yours NOW!

Become part of this On-line community today!

Find out why 20 million people use the Internet and learn how to connect to various personal and business resources, activities, organizations and services around the world.

See details for your FREE ISSUE

Internet *WORLD* magazine

FREE ISSUE Voucher

☐ **YES!** Rush me my FREE ISSUE of Internet World. If I like what I see I will pay your one-year invoice for just $24.95, a savings of 50% off the newsstand cover price!

If I decide not to subscribe, I will simply write "cancel" across your invoice, return it and owe nothing. The FREE issue is mine to keep no matter what I decide.

SY-30594BF

Name _____

Address _____

City _____

State _____ Zip _____

Online Users... Save 50% Today!

You save 50% off the newsstand price right now when you sign up for a subscription to **Online Access** magazine, the first magazine to bring you complete coverage of the online world.

Every issue of **Online Access** brings you the best, the fastest, the smartest and the most economical ways to grab the thousands of opportunities that are available to you online.

If you want information about:
- The Internet
- Investment Services
- Major Online Services
- E-Mail
- Information Databases
- Bulletin Board Services
- Wireless Communication
- Anything and everything that you need to do online...

Online Access *magazine is your one stop choice.*

Subscribe today and sign up for a one year, 10 issue subscription for only $24.75*, a savings of 50% off the newsstand price! Simply fill out the information below and send it in today.

Your subscription is risk-free...if you're not completely satisfied with **Online Access**, you may cancel at any time and receive a refund of any unmailed copies.

Name_____ Title_____

Company_____

Address_____

City_____ State____ Zip_____

Daytime Phone_____ OA1

❏ Check Enclosed.   ❏ Bill Me.

Mail to: Online Access, 5615 W. Cermak Rd., Chicago, IL 60650-2290 or subscribe by:
Fax: 708-656-1990 • Voice: 800-36-MODEM a • E-mail: 74604.2001.compuserve.com or readoa.aol.com
Make sure you mention this ad and "OA1" to receive your special rate.

* *Canadian subs $24.75; all other countries $87.15. U.S. Funds Only. Prices are subject to change.*

Online Access®

What's on the Disk?
Everything You Need!

With the help of this disk, you can begin to enjoy the Internet *IMMEDIATELY!* On this disk you'll find:

NetCruiser, a program that will connect any Windows 3.1 or better PC, equipped with a 9600 baud or faster modem, directly to the Internet over an ordinary phone line. **NetCruiser** also gives you:

◆ **A Friendly Windows Interface**, giving you an intuitively simple and familiar way to use the Internet.

◆ **A Versatile and Easy-to-Use E-Mail System**, allowing you to communicate with over 15 million Internet users.

◆ **A Usenet News Reader**, giving you the ability to stay up-to-date on the latest gossip, opinions, information, and more...on just about any topic imaginable.

◆ **Two Information Browsing Programs (gopher and World Wide Web)**, allowing you to search the world to find the information and topics you want fast.

◆ **The Internet's File Transfer Protocol (FTP)**, allowing you to easily download a wide range of software, games, graphics, and other useful files.

◆ **Telnet**, giving you the ability to access and use computers all over the world from the privacy of your own home.

NetCruiser provides these services at remarkable savings. You'll get:

◆ Your own personal e-mail address and mailbox on the Internet.

◆ **40 Hours** per month of access to the Internet via **Netcom**, a leading Internet service provider, during prime time (between 9 A.M. and midnight) at **No Charge**.

◆ **Unlimited free access to the Internet on weekends** and between midnight and 9 A.M.

All for just a $25.00 registration fee and $19.95 per month. (Additional hours during prime time will be charged at *only $2.00 per hour.*) As a purchaser of this book, you'll also get a unique Registration Number, allowing you to take advantage of a **Special Offer**. You'll get:

◆ **One month** of Netcom service **absolutely free!** (The $19.95 charge for your first month as described above will be waived.)

Taking advantage of this offer will give you the use of a large number of local telephone numbers spread all over the U.S., which maximizes the chance that, **for the price of a local phone call, you can**...

Access the Internet!